Barbara Haselbach   Dance Education

Barbara Haselbach

Dance Education

Basic principles and models
for Nursery and Primary School

Edition 11351
ISBN 0 901938 11 4

Schott & Co. Ltd.
48 Gt. Marlborough Street,
London W1V 2BN

© 1971 Ernst Klett Verlag, Stuttgart, Bundesrepublik Deutschland
English Translation by Margaret Murray © 1978 Schott & Co. Ltd., London
Photographs: Willi Moegle
Edition No. 11351
ISBN 0 901938 11 4

Contents

Part Four: Survey of material according to age groups

Part Five: Lesson examples

Preface

Dance education comprises elements of both physical and aesthetic education. Its medium of expression is the movement of the human body which should be developed and differentiated. It is therefore closely connected with physical education. Over and above this dance education transmits the aesthetic and communicative aspects of dance. To these belong the general sensitisation and development of creative and social behaviour through improvisation and composition as well as through the reproduction and interpretation of various dance forms. These elements are valid for the individual and for the group; they produce possibilities for expression that are characteristic for both.

This book has grown out of many years' work with Orff-Schulwerk, an educational idea that is founded upon the recognition that dance, language and music represent an original and integrated form of expression. In early childhood, even today, the child nearly always expresses himself through a unity of language, movement and sound.

In contrast to other 'pure' methods of dance education this book will very often show the relationship of movement to music, to language and poetry, as well as to pictorial or dramatic ideas or objects. Not least because, in the wide realm of general education as well as in the specific realm of aesthetic education an ever more strongly felt tendency is developing, not to isolate subjects from one another but rather to express themes of general significance that will involve a combination of subjects.

It is the intention of this book in the first place to give colleagues without professional dance training some stimulation for working with dance education for children from four to ten years old both inside and outside the school. Any fixation upon a particular method has been avoided; the broadest possible foundation should be the prerequisite for a subsequent specialisation (modern dance, folk or social dancing, jazz). Such specialisation, however, as well as the careful nursing and cultivation of exceptional talent, should in all circumstances be entrusted only to the professional dance teacher.

Besides offering an indication of the aims, purpose and content of dance education, together with material and examples for the teacher interested in dance, this book also seeks to give colleagues some new, individual points of view, or, at all events, points of departure for professional discussion.

In the interest of general understanding the use of any of the current forms of dance notation has been avoided. This has presented many problems, since certain movements can often only be approximately described.

I acknowledge the help given by all my teachers and friends in preparing me for the task of writing this book. I thank Carl Orff and Gunild Keetman who gave the original impetus. I also thank all children, students and colleagues from the Orff Institute in Salzburg, as well as those in other countries with whom I have been allowed to work, for their indirect help, and I thank Hermann Regner for his encouragement. I am very indebted to Margaret Murray for her tireless assistance in bringing about the existence of an English edition.

Salzburg
Spring 1973

Translator's note

Terminology in the field of dance, education and music has its variations from one part of the English-speaking world to another. There are also some words that have a special meaning in this book. I have therefore felt it necessary to provide an explanation of some terms and expressions in a short glossary which can be found on page 211.

I should like to record my gratitude to Francine Watson Coleman, who has given me advice on dance terminology and invaluable help with the problem of describing movement as precisely as possible but with a clear and economic use of words.

M.M.

Fundamental considerations
Part One

Survey of various types of dance and movement training

In many countries and at certain times the dance fulfils very diverse functions that are dependent upon cultural, social, psychological, political and other factors. The dance can be a ritual, an inducement to ecstasy, a recreational pleasure, a social convention, a child's game or a form of public entertainment. This book deals exclusively with the educational aspects of dancing for a specific age group. For clarity of definition and in order to see the material that comes into consideration, the most important types of dance and movement training are outlined in a brief introduction.

Classical ballet

This originated in the sixteenth century mainly from court dances and evolved into a form of public performance whose movements and rules were later developed and classified. The name 'ballet' that has long been in use, has today been extended to cover all dances performed on the stage.

The training of a classical ballet dancer requires many years and should start as early as possible (between the ages of about four and six). The movements are stylised and predetermined and offer the child no opportunity to develop his own imagination or creativity. Further, since reliable tuition can only be given by specialists it cannot be taught in normal schools, but must be left to special boarding schools or ballet schools outside the school education system.

Modern dance

Modern dance began in America and Germany in the twentieth century as a protest against the rigidity of the classical ballet of that time. It allows much scope for improvisation; its content and forms have strongly influenced modern stage dancing so that in many countries it has become a kind of synthesis of classical and modern dance.

In its present form, and especially in the way it has developed in America, it, too, requires a strict and sophisticated 'adult technique' whose elements do not suit a child's mentality. On the other hand, fundamental and creative dancing is suitable for children as a preparation for modern dance.

Ethnic dance

By ethnic dances one means folk dances of other races and cultures that very often have a ritual aspect (e.g. Indian, Balinese and voodoo dances). The study of these dances by foreigners demands many years of research and also a thorough understanding of the customs and culture of the people concerned. Ethnic dances are excluded from school dance education in order to avoid their superficial misuse. The content of such dances is generally beyond the understanding of children in the age group under consideration.

Folk dance

This term generally describes anonymous dances from various countries. Music, content, movements and forms as well as costumes are dependent upon conditions in the respective countries. Despite their national characteristics the dance material is 'international' and in many cases suitable for children. Some of the simplest folk dances can therefore be most suitable for the children within our age range.

Historical dance

Dances of the high society of the past are included under the title 'historical' or 'court' dances. Many of these, such as the 'branle' for instance, are still known today—in slightly altered form—as children's or round dances. They are best suited to the secondary school (showing interrelation between music history, history of art and literature) but at the age of eight or nine children can start with the simpler ones.

Contredanses

These originate in the old English country dances with their 'longways sets' and 'rounds'; they came to the European continent via France towards the middle of the seventeenth century. The English Folk Dance and Song Society is engaged in their revival and in a new interpretation of the famous collection by John Playford. One or two examples of these are suitable for the secondary school.

Square dances

The American square dance has incorporated extensive motifs from European (e.g. English, Irish, Scottish, French and German) dances. An attempt to regenerate this form of dance started in 1930, conceiving it as a recreation for all ages, all social strata and both sexes. The respective dance formations known as 'square' (a cross of four pairs), 'circle' (pairs in a circle) and 'contra' (two rows facing each other) are called out by a 'caller'. This style of dancing is quick and jolly and can occasionally be used—in its simpler forms—with nine to ten year olds.

Social dances (ball room dancing)

The name is not very appropriate since all dances were mostly developed by a particular social stratum. Originally they were developed from folk dances (Viennese waltz, tango). Today they have become increasingly commercialised and new fashions appear every year. The standard dances with dancers holding each other closely in pairs are too sophisticated for the young children dealt with in this book, in spite of experiments to the contrary. The simplest dances in row formation or—as popular today—free, will doubtless give much enjoyment to children of about nine years. For older children the skilful use of modern social dances can be highly recommended. In many American schools so-called 'social dancing' is included in the school curriculum.

Jazz dancing

Under this name a style of dancing imported into Europe from Africa and Afro-America is understood. Its movements are fundamentally different from those of the European dance styles. The jazz dance has increasingly been gaining more ground in amateur and professional dance circles. Young people undoubtedly have a great interest in jazz dancing which should, however, be taught by a fully trained teacher.

Beat and pop dancing

Beat and pop dancing also possess the characteristic features of African Negro dancing. Many youngsters dance beat and pop without having been taught. These dances should not be left out of any dancing activity with young people. Practical experience of the inclusion of beat dances in the education of four to ten year olds does not yet appear to exist.

Gymnastics

This is a form of physical training the aim of which is the cultivation of human movement through the development, intensification and preservation of individual aptitudes. For this purpose apparatus can be used. Rhythmic, dance and curative gymnastics, as well as that used as a preparatory training for a specific kind of sport (e.g. ski-gymnastics), are special branches.

Eurhythmy

An art of movement, created by Rudolf Steiner and fostered in anthroposophy, which attempts to express ideas through inspired physical movements as a kind of 'visible language'. It is taught as an artistic form of expression (emphatically independent from pantomime and dance), as sound and tone eurhythmy, but beyond this also as therapeutic eurhythmy.

Eurhythmics, rhythmic education

At the beginning of the twentieth century the music educator Emile Jaques-Dalcroze strove to establish a kind of 'total method' to overcome the isolation of intellectual and spiritual functions from physical ones. By rhythmic education, a teaching method in which the combined unfolding of human capacities is governed by rhythmic principles is understood. These ideas can be realised mainly in music education but also in rhythmic gymnastics. They are especially effective in therapeutical training and for teaching in special schools.

Creative Educational Dance

'Creative Educational Dance' is based on the work of Rudolf von Laban, whose ideas are spread mainly in England, in some Scandinavian countries and--in adapted form--also in America. The main emphasis falls here on the child's individual experiments in movement, his capacity for expression being extended by Laban's sixteen 'movement themes'. The role of the traditional dance forms is here subordinate; the relations with drama and dance-drama are close.

Fundamental dance education

This is based and built upon the child's movements. Education in music and in movement are intimately connected and there is a close relationship with language. Besides learning the basic principles of dance and music, personal, creative activity is of prime importance. The creative as well as the gymnastic and musical prerequisites for a transition to other disciplines (modern dance, folk and historical dance etc.) are provided.

The combination of dance, music and language

Those forms of human expression that encompass dance, music and language in an original form, are found in their most genuine state in children and primitive peoples. The causes for such expression can vary, but ultimately they arise from tensions of emotional, intellectual or physical kinds that are released through rhythmically stressed or flowing-swinging movements. The movements are intensified through language, through song and also through instrumental accompaniment. In primitive civilisations we find no evidence of exhibitionist intentions at this stage, music and dance being rather a happening of cultic origin and content that gives a sense of fulfilment to those who participate in it.

Dancing, at this stage, is equivalent to music making; through the rhythmic sound of the steps, through spontaneous shouts and repeated invocations that develop into songs. The rhythm of the dance is stressed through the jingling of the dancers' ornaments (chains, belts, earrings and bangles made of bones, shells and hollow fruits), through the stamping of feet and banging of sticks and through hand-clapping or slapping various parts of the body. Primitive instruments of earlier civilisations are also used (drums of every type and other percussion instruments, flutes and similar wind instruments made of wood, cane or bone and simple string instruments).

The dances, accompanied in this way, can demonstrate pictorially in pantomime a real event with its desired ending; speech and song can also be added to form an early dramatic play. On the other hand there is the basic type of dance that is not pictorial, that has no imitative elements and finds its expression in an abstract form of movement motifs that are varied in space, dynamics and rhythm.

In the comparative studies of musicologists, ethnologists and anthropologists we find detailed descriptions of such 'total' performances--combining music, dance and language--that differ individually very much but that often present certain similarities: that the inhabitants of a village or the members of a tribe participate in such dances while the children also dance at the end of a long line or in a circle of their own. In this way the children grow up in the dance tradition of their own people. Dances, whose themes are considered unsuitable for their age, are taboo and children have to undergo special initiation rites before being allowed to watch or take part in them. Very often these communal dances are accompanied by singing, clapping or by playing on simple instruments (e.g. all kinds of rattles and castanets) that are appropriate to the movements. A dance orchestra is often placed at the edge of the dancing area. When a dancer is tired he will join it and play, sing or accompany the others with clapping and with encouraging shouts. Even today it is still possible to see this lively exchange of roles between playing and dancing, and sometimes also the combination of both, in those folk dances which have not yet become a mere tourist attraction.

Language undergoes a transformation in its relation to dancing. For use with dancing and rhythmically accentuated movements the words are placed according to the lengths of their syllables so that the word and movement rhythms coincide. The dance song developed from the combination of articulated movement and melodic speech. While originally the meaning of the text stood in closest relationship to the dance—as we can still see in some children's singing games—we later also find examples in which the rhythm of the language initiates the movements without those movements providing an interpretation of the text.

In the course of their historical development each art form evolved increasingly in its own right. Music—especially in the Western world—has moved further and further towards 'absolute' music. Language freed itself from its cultic relationship to music and dance and evolved into independent poetry. Dance also became an independent art form, but, because of its nature, remained the one that could least of all be entirely detached from its sister arts. Today all three art forms still meet—or rather they meet again—in two fields, in the theatre and in dance music. In the theatre all these arts have co-operated, at least from time to time, since the Renaissance. Opera needs words and often includes dance; drama often employs stage music and movement in pantomimes or dances—though not always in integrated form. In ballet, more precisely in dance for the theatre, music and artistically devised movements complement each other. Even words—whether poems or fragments of everyday slogans—are sometimes included in modern choreography. The second meeting point is dance music. This category includes the music of court dances, country dances and modern social dances as well as folk dances. Here music and dance have influenced one another reciprocally. The words, which were originally of a relatively high literary importance as text for the dance tune, have receded in the course of time more and more into the background and today they exist only in danced folk songs or in modern light music.

There exists therefore a form of performance that unites dance, music and language in balanced relationship. Besides this their interpenetration can be seen in many instances of everyday life.

From observing very young children we know that they utter sounds when making early attempts at moving. They do this not only in order to draw attention to themselves, but also as if to try out and to exercise voice and limbs in play. When a baby is rocked to sleep, if its mother sings or speaks to it in a soothing, melodious voice, the child is quietened and lulled to sleep both by the movement of the rocking and by the undulating pattern of speech or melody. The effect is similar when frightened children huddle together in a corner or in bed and hum softly to themselves while making slightly swinging, almost rocking movements.

We can pick out some movement games played by slightly older children as relevant in this connection. We all know the kind of hopscotch that is practised according to a strict set of rules that are handed down from child to child, with specific steps and turns, hopping on one or both feet over a pattern drawn on the ground. It is especially when children play alone that they often sing or hum a song or an improvised tune that corresponds to the rhythm of their movements or subordinates them to the melody.

In places where music has not become a mere background noise, where children still prick up their ears when music is played, it often happens that they are unable·to sit still; they fidget, spring to their feet and start to dance in their own way. Who has not yet seen, when a procession passes through the town, how the children march right behind the band or run alongside it on the kerb, inventing their own dance steps with exuberant joy? Similarly the occasions when, in imitation of adults, they start dancing to music on the radio, often with better results and with more invention than their elders. The pleasure they derive from this dancing is visible on their faces, for this spontaneity is not yet hidden behind the mask of convention. Even adults when they hear music on the radio or at a concert begin, almost imperceptibly, to move. They beat time with their feet, their fingers or with their head, or sway slightly with the whole body to and fro. This often somewhat ridiculous, but for us adults most significant phenomenon, is basically nothing else but a kind of rudimentary, stunted dance movement which, thanks to conventional upbringing, we have ceased to be able to express in any other way. We no longer dance like children when we feel the inclination, but only when circumstances, dictated by social behaviour, offer us the opportunity.

There are other cases in which, consciously or unconsciously, the effect of music comes into use: work songs, marching music and workers' songs. In earlier times many manual labours were co-ordinated through an accompaniment of rhythmic speech. In many cases the rhythmic chant became a song (e.g. when lifting or pulling heavy objects, when rowing, when pulling nets or boats ashore). 'Shanties' for instance, were originally sailors' work songs. In processions, parades, long marches and even walks, movement is influenced by music (more often songs in these cases). Nowadays music is heard in factories, very often in supermarkets and stores, one could say almost constantly, where it is being used to stimulate the willingness to work and to buy.

These observations demonstrate that music exercises a great influence upon movement. Through being carried along by the dynamics of the music, the movement generally appears to be less tiring. Through the rhythm of the music the timing of the movement is organised. The emotional content of the music distracts the attention from physical exertion; the pleasure in performance is increased and the entire movement becomes more accomplished and intensive. On the other hand, a continuously repeated movement very often releases in man, through its inherent rhythm, music that expresses itself in rhythmic speech, singing, humming, whistling or sound-producing gestures (clapping, finger-snapping, thigh-slapping and stamping).

Resulting from these observations it follows that for teaching purposes, especially in the nursery school and in the first two years of normal schooling, the unity of movement, music and language must be preserved, for example as it is intended and presented in Orff-Schulwerk. The strong influence of music upon movement and dance is valid, however, for all age groups. Music and move-

19

ment should be employed on equal terms according to their own individual laws.

In both fields children should be guided towards the acquisition of basic experience and understanding, the emphasis being placed sometimes on movement, sometimes on music.

The development of the child's
basic powers of movement

How does the rich variety of a child's movement, upon which his dance and movement education is based, develop? How does a child gain sufficient assurance and experience to be able to move in both familiar and unfamiliar surroundings, alone or in company with others in play, work and dance?

The fact that movement activity plays a decisive role both in the physical and mental development of the child should neither be overlooked nor undervalued. It is well-known that, compared with other mammals, the new-born human baby comes into the world unprepared and helpless and entirely dependent upon others. It takes a baby a year or more to master the upright position. The preliminary stages for this are lying, lifting the head and later creeping and crawling on the stomach. In the second half of his first year a baby learns to sit up without help, soon after to stand and later to move carefully from one place to another. In her book *Der Tanz als Bewegungsphänomen* Dorothee Günther calls the mastering of the upright position one of 'mankind's great "miracles of becoming" '. (*)

The sense of balance is essential to acquiring the upright position. Without it both the upright position and all the movements dependent on it would be impossible. The more self-assured the posture, the more the arms and hands are free for other tasks. Seizing and grasping also belong to a stage of development that a child achieves through constant and untiring practice. An adult can do much to help and encourage by playing with the child and by providing material and playthings.

From the second year onwards a child develops his capacity for locomotion. The first of these is walking, which reaches maturity in terms of dynamics when the child is eight to ten years old; a distinction between walking and running is first formed at the beginning of the third year. The relatively difficult co-ordination of skipping and jumping can also not be expected before this age. The time span of a child's development is individually determined by physical constitution, by the attention and help he receives from his parents or guardians, and by the stimulus given by such things as playgrounds and material objects. Generally speaking, by the beginning of his fourth year a child has learned to master the basic principles of locomotion and—from this moment on— is also able and ready to learn to differentiate, vary and combine them in dance

Der Tanz als Bewegungsphänomen, Hamburg 1962, p. 28

and in all branches of movement education.

In his first years a child acquires the major part of all movement experiences that he will encounter in his whole life. The transition from a helpless lying position, in which he is totally dependent on his environment, to walking, running, jumping, turning, climbing, clambering, swimming, falling, stretching and contracting, balancing and rolling on the floor, is extremely rich in experience and establishes the child's relationship to his environment and to his fellow human beings.

Every challenge is an experiment: the distance from the chair leg to mother's arms, a door and what lies behind it, a flight of stairs that is so difficult to ascend and descend and that leads to an unknown world, children to play with and to hold by the hand.

All this is connected with physical and psychical experiences that provide contact with objects and people and that stimulate the child's curiosity and initiate the processes of learning and cognition.

Play and movement, released by internal or external stimuli, are vital for development. Through this activity and his physical reactions to it the child learns those movements he needs in daily life: the movement qualities of speed, strength, agility, stamina, dexterity and precision becoming more and more developed. In addition he discovers new ways of moving that may appear without purpose to an adult. He wants to walk on tiptoe or on his heels, he tries to stand on his head, to walk on his hands, to turn somersaults, to balance on kerbstones or on low walls, he spins round and round until he stumbles and falls, and in so doing is happy and content. He hops over stones and splashes in puddles, jumps over areas marked out according to his own rules. The spatial possibilities of the playground are exploited, he runs round the trees, experiments with zig-zag lines, forms chains and circles, and runs in angles and curves along the paths of parks and gardens. He invents games with others and tests himself in all kinds of 'tricks' that will strengthen his self-assurance.

A child is also fascinated by the repetition of a certain movement, its duration and its possibilities for rhythmic variation. He performs his hops and runs, turns and jumps in various free-rhythmic versions. An order is often established by means of a little tune sung as an accompaniment, an improvised, hummed melody or a spoken text. Together with other children little songs are danced or scenes are acted (play-acting). Through his own experiments and also through imitation a child learns the various forms of traditional games and customs and the movements for dances.

Skipping, tripping along, running, spinning round and other ways of moving favoured by children are indications of an intensified, joyous awareness of life, but also of a surplus energy that must eventually express itself in a more or less intense motor activity.

Play and movement for today's children

Up to the start of nursery school a child learns mainly with the help of his parents or guardians, but also on his own account or through his contact with other children. The more opportunities for play offered by adults the more a child will gain in skill, assurance and self-confidence, the more he will move freely and without inhibition. This will provide the best prerequisite for a progressive dance and movement education. The opportunities for play are unfortunately becoming less and less adequate in the living space available for today's children. In flats that are mostly very small there is insufficient space; the child is furthermore prevented from making a noise out of consideration for the neighbours or landlord. Laughing, calling and shouting, however, are all ways of expressing the intensity of play. When all these activities are constantly suppressed, when all noisy and lively games are forbidden by parents--often unwillingly--the spontaneity of play inevitably suffers.

Playrooms and playgrounds are available in only very few apartment blocks. Public playgrounds are rare, especially in big cities. They are often too far from home; the children cannot make their way alone through the traffic and their mothers seldom have time to take them and to wait for them there. Such playgrounds are also only in rare cases adequately equipped for younger children. One climbing frame standing on concrete will not necessarily create the right atmosphere for play. When children have to curtail their spontaneous, joyful movements and inventions both at home and on playgrounds, when these negative tendencies have to be 'untaught' in even the very young, the ensuing reactions will express themselves in various contradictory types of behaviour: children will come to school or nursery school partly inhibited in their movements, shy and passive; others will discharge their pent-up energy in almost uncontrollable boisterousness. These children can neither fit into a community nor accept the rules of a game.

Individual countries cater for this need for movement in children within the curriculum of nursery and primary schools with varying degrees of understanding and open-mindedness. Games, eurhythmics, drill and gymnastics, creative dance--all these are mentioned. All come under the general heading of 'movement education'. Curricula only rarely give precise instructions on the choice of teaching material. (*) It is particularly the instructions relating to dance education that are mostly scanty and are restricted to mentioning a few songs and games that could be performed as circle dances. Later on, at best,

*This and the following seven sentences applies more to the situation in German-speaking countries.

square dances and folk dances are added. In the majority of cases examples of games and dances are given which the children have to learn step by step.

It is hardly ever a question of using the medium of movement as a form of creative expression for the child. Instructions and suggestions on how to procure the children's own ideas and solutions to given tasks are very rarely found in school curricula, and the possibility of teaching in such a way is often not even mentioned. Although psychologists and educationalists have long pointed out the dangers inherent in a system of learning that is based solely upon imitation, in practice this warning is rarely heeded. The type of movement education in which both teacher and pupil share a creative role is a rare occurrence.

In comparison with Great Britain or America dance education plays a very minor role in the schools of German-speaking countries. In many schools it is either discounted or is allotted much too small a portion of movement education time. There can be several reasons for this neglect:

1. There is still a tendency to consider dance education as a luxury and therefore as an out-of-school activity.

The early experience and practice of movement must be encouraged by the school for other opportunities hardly exist, unless especially far-sighted and wealthy parents provide such an education for their children outside the school. The development of abilities, however, should not depend upon the social position of the parents, nor upon the possibility of their having little or no understanding or interest in this field. Just as every child has the opportunity and the right to acquire the so-called basic, cultural techniques of reading, writing and arithmetic as part of his fundamental education, so he should also be given the opportunity of exercising his powers of imagination, his need for expression and his creative abilities in music, painting, craft and dancing. Movement is a medium of expression as are language, music, form and colour. Its instrument, the body, needs cultivation and practice like any other instrument.

Neglect of this educational field produces inhibition, undeveloped powers of expression, movement shyness and all the related psychological and physical harms and conflicts. In watching adolescents we can see relatively often how a bottled-up need for movement takes effect.

2. It is rare for general teachers to feel competent to teach dance and movement and this is usually why they opt out of it.

Since not all colleges where teachers are trained provide dance education as a main subject, it is not surprising that young teachers are unfamiliar with the practical work, material and methodology involved. Dance education should be taught on a much broader basis by qualified teachers in all teacher training institutions. It should be included in the comprehensive field of movement education and be particularly connected with musical education, that is to say, music teachers, in co-operation with dance teachers, should take charge of such aspects as movement accompaniment.

3. It is very often argued that sport education gives sufficient scope for the movement needs of children and makes adequate provision for movement training—that dance education is therefore superfluous.

Even in professional circles it is not absolutely clear, in spite of the exemplary work of some authors, that movement education must also include its artistic aspects. The purpose of this comprehensive field of education cannot be confined to the development of the highest abilities in sport and to training recruits for athletic contests. It is at least equally important to bring to fruition the child's imaginative capacity and his concept of form. Dance education with children and adolescents must be seen as both physical and aesthetic-artistic education; it furthers not only the development and capacity for achievement of the individual, but also provides outstanding assistance in the field of communication.

4. In practice teachers and headmasters blame the neglect of dance and movement education onto lack of rooms, instruments, teaching manuals and the children's lack of interest.

It is true that there are only very few specialist books in German on this subject, but essential stimuli can be found in the foreign (and especially English) literature now available in this field. The lack of training has already been discussed. Most schools are equipped with musical instruments. The teachers who know how to use them appropriately, however, are missing. Lack of interest on the part of the children is usually the result of the negative attitude of teachers and parents; as long as they have no experience of this subject their indifference can only be regarded as an accepted prejudice. In this, as in all other subjects, the children's interest depends upon the teacher's ability to arouse it. The difficulties of organisation will be dealt with in a later chapter.

Finally, every teacher should be prepared to inform herself about the aims, organisation and teaching methods to be found in other countries, particularly in those that are more advanced than her own.

Curriculum for dance education in nursery and primary schools

Dance education belongs to the field of aesthetic education. It strives, through movement, to bring to expression and fruition the physical, emotional and intellectual capacities of the child. Its aims therefore include:

a) education through movement and dance
b) introduction to, and preparation for a creative and artistic form of dancing, hence education for dance.

These tasks are closely connected: a) forms the basis upon which b) can—if broadly extended—be made accessible to all children or can be intensified in special courses for the especially gifted (dance study groups, dance lessons out of school, special training colleges).

The experiences gained through movement have a fundamental effect on the general development of the child's personality, but become more specialised in content only through further development and intensification.

In the following paragraphs the aspects which make up a curriculum for dance education are briefly outlined in both their general and specific aims:

The discovery of the body's capacity for movement

Quite a long period of time for physical development is needed before the child realises that his body consists of various parts and before he learns to move these arbitrarily and in isolation. Sensitivity and control increase by degrees and so does the awareness of the infinite scope for variety. This variety is dependent upon functional conditions and upon the various ways of moving in terms of space, time and dynamics depending on the movement motivation. The cultivation of movement capacity must provide tasks in which the child has, on the one hand, to find and try out new, unexplored movements, while on the other hand he is allowed to continue practising what he has learned, and to exploit this for new and varied uses.

Co-ordination

The training of co-ordination in movement forms an important part of movement education. Through frequent practice individual parts of the body have to learn to work together; the difficulty increases the more the movements differ. The arms and legs, for instance, can have contrasting speeds or rhythms, can move in opposite directions, or can differ in flow or emphasis. In addition, co-ordination between music and movement and between pairs or groups that are executing movements together must be observed and practised.

Orientation and awareness of space

With increasing physical awareness, the position of the body in a given space and its relationship to other objects in space becomes clearer. A child learns to judge distances, to adjust his path of travel in relation to those of others, to avoid obstacles, to distinguish one direction from another and to recognise various groupings. He experiences that the whole body, or parts of it, can move through space in various directions and at various levels and he learns to adapt his movements to the spatial conditions. He eventually becomes able to find his bearings in an empty room as well as in one filled with people, and also within the framework of different group formations. Adjustment to a particular side of the room or to a partner can follow or it can be omitted. The growing security in this field shows itself in the way the children move in everyday life as well as in their dance lessons.

Assistance for movement-inhibited and hyperactive children

In every class there are children who are conspicuous because of their hyperactive restlessness or movement shyness and inhibition. The teacher should try to find out whether such behaviour is caused by an excitable nature, by an unstable phase of developmental change or by some illness. In the latter case the child might—with medical advice—seek special treatment.

External discipline has a merely deceptive effect on the movement of the child that is hyperactive. Such children have a very strong need for movement that must be satisfied as far as possible. They must learn, however, to fit into the community and not to disturb unduly either the other children or the lesson. They have to learn gradually to control their motor activity and to understand the necessity for this. Their own insight, their own will and not the 'you must'—the pressure from the teacher—should induce this change of behaviour.

The children who are very inhibited in their movements are at the other extreme. As long as this inhibition is not specifically psychological or physiological in origin (a decision for a specialist), some special attention from the teacher and the giving of individual exercises can be helpful. The experience of frequent small achievements can spur these children on to an intensified participation. Excessive demands and repeated failure are particularly discouraging and therefore dangerous.

Training the senses

Training the senses, intensifying perception and the ability to give form to these perceptions and to analyse them critically as an individual or as a member of a group, is one of the most significant and predominant tasks in aesthetic education. Opportunities for this are lacking in our world that every day becomes more dull and abstract. Impressions received through the senses form the invaluable raw material for all aesthetic (and not only aesthetic) experiences that are made conscious and given form.

In dance education it is a question of stimulating the senses that, directly or indirectly, have something to do with movement (of the body) and also with executing these movements in a given space, with other children, possibly to an accompaniment and with the inclusion of material objects or other aids. The senses concerned are:

a) kinaesthetic
b) balance
c) sight
d) hearing
e) touch

a) *kinaesthetic sense*

This gives us information about the amount of tension in muscles and tendons and locates the position of joints. It is sometimes also described as muscular sense or sense of posture. To bring what we perceive through this sense to consciousness involves learning to feel whether the body or individual parts of it are tense or relaxed and to locate their current posture. The control of these sensations is an important factor for all assured and consciously actuated movement.

b) *sense of balance*

The labyrinths of the inner ear are the seat of a sense of balance as well as of hearing. In movement education it is above all the awareness of direction and change of direction and the perception of variations in speed that are important.

c) *sense of sight*

The eye allows us to comprehend the space in which we move; it helps us to find the partner or the group with whom we wish to dance; it provides optical stimuli that can become a dance-like inspiration; it allows us to see the dancing of others and to recognise and appreciate lines and forms. In training this sense, simple tasks (who is moving, in which direction, which part of the body?) become more and more differentiated (e.g. is the movement symmetrical or not, slow or accelerating, does the hand or the elbow lead? etc.) until a movement is precisely understood in terms of space, time and dynamics. This ability is a necessary prerequisite for all movement accompaniment. Another task which involves this sense is the observation and recognition of faults in the performance of others.

d) *sense of hearing*

Here we consider the beginnings of aural training, of listening to, distinguishing and naming the many sounds around us. Pitch, duration, intensity and tone colour are established, produced by the children themselves and identified. Simple rhythmic and melodic structures should be recognised and reproduced.

Simple unison melodies and also the simplest forms of polyphony should be introduced. Tonic Solfa and French time names will be helpful. The further development of ear training will be taken over by music education.

e) *sense of touch*

Touching the floor or other parts of the room, apparatus or material objects, a partner or one's own body with varying degrees of intensity must be experienced. The surface and the shape, the temperature and the consistency can be felt. Pressure and counterpressure, character and form should be recognised in touching and feeling and the impressions received then reproduced in a personal form.

Concentration

Parents and schools are complaining more and more about children's lack of concentration. This weakness is only too easy to understand when we consider the many and often contrasting impressions to which children are subjected every day. Lack of concentration is mostly not a sign of lack of interest, but is caused by the disturbing after effects of too many undigested impressions. The intensive pursuit of the same theme over a fairly long period of time should be practised. In movement education and in its relationship with music there are exercises that constantly introduce slight variations, so that the children are apparently being faced with new problems though they are in fact working within the same theme. Periods of intense concentration should be short and should be interspersed with pauses for relaxation. The attention can be equally well focussed on the control and skill of one's own body as on the unexpected reaction of a partner, on the approach of a ball or on different qualities in the musical accompaniment (duration or pitch, intensity, formal structure, recognition of a theme). A quiet atmosphere in the room avoids unnecessary distraction. It is only sensible to allow tasks to finish naturally and not to stop them abruptly (e.g. tracing the path a partner took in the room; finishing the movement together with the fading out of the music; observing a movement that is becoming smaller and smaller and that comes to rest; quietly waiting until everyone has finished their task). Exercises in concentration can be intensified by means of acoustical, visual and imaginative stimuli.

Memory

Memory is to a great extent dependent upon various impressions. In dance education it is mainly the motor, acoustic and visual memory that is being trained. Only through classifying the sequence of single factors that constitute the elements of a dance, whether individually or group designed, is it possible to repeat the movements concerned and to transmit them to others. The capacity to remember a movement sequence and thus be able to repeat it is helped in various ways: through its relation to music, through an inherent sense of timing, through a specific disposition within the available space and through the physical sensations stimulated by the movement itself. Memory proficiency can be trained, otherwise it would be impossible to explain how dancers are able to remember complicated sequences of very different dances and dance roles.

In music as well as in language and dance, respective notations are used to support the memory. The different types of dance notation (Laban-Kinetography, Benesh-Notation) are generally too complicated for children and laymen. For them simple symbols can replace more difficult notation, sketches can help the remembering of positions, directions of travel and individual shapes.

Reaction

Each movement that is prompted by an inner or outer stimulus is considered as a reaction. In dance and movement education reactions, mainly to acoustic and visual, more rarely to tactile stimuli, are practised. The meaning of such stimuli must be recognised and transformed into more or less personal motor responses within the framework of the exercise concerned. Practice of this kind develops concentration and attention; it creates an association between the stimulus and its meaning and requires a quick decision on how to respond to it. The value of the exercise, however, does not lie in producing the fastest reaction to an unvarying stimulus, but in the adaptation to ever-changing situations, each of which requires a specific attitude.

Social behaviour

Movement education offers opportunities for developing social behaviour that are particularly numerous and favourable. In the many exercises that children try out simultaneously though independently, they have to learn not to hinder or disturb others but nevertheless at the same time to find enough space in which to perform their own task. In tasks with partners or in groups a joint solution depends to a high degree on the attention paid to each other while moving and while working with apparatus or instruments, and on the response and the adaptation to the others' capacities. Especially when leading a group the leader should try to make sure that every member of his group has time and room to follow him. When working at small, group compositions, each child should be offered the opportunity to contribute his suggestions but, when this situation arises, he should also learn to submit to an idea put forward by others which is considered more suitable at that particular moment. The more independent from her the children become in learning to work together, the more the teacher may assume a purely advisory role in such exercises.

Communication

Lack of personal contact and breakdown in communication is given today as the reason for the isolation of many people. In school it is also inhibition, anxiety or mistrust that make it difficult for children to make contact with others. We do not yet know how the school of the future with its variable methods of streaming, of isolating work in the teaching laboratory and its other new working methods will influence the ability of children and adolescents to communicate.

Since the earliest times communal dancing has been the outstanding means for the forming of communities (the history of dance and culture provides countless examples). That this kind of dancing should not be enforced but should be performed voluntarily goes without saying and justifies the establishment of working communities. Dancing together produces different effects. The joy of a common activity and the feeling of belonging to a community predominate in the communal performance of traditional dances. In creating and developing new dance forms the participants learn both the difficulties of producing a group composition and ways of solving such difficulties. Both these experiences further communication.

Creativity

Creativity is understood in the sense of modern research as the creative coming to grips with one's environment. Children should be stimulated to practise it and be encouraged themselves to recognise problems and to find new and individual solutions to them. Spontaneous ideas for specific tasks could lead, through emphasis on various aspects of the problem, to a countless number of solutions and conclusions. Divergent thinking, which does not uncritically accept standardised forms and examples, and which does not strive for the 'one and only solution' but, on the contrary, dares to attempt new and untried possibilities and produces a great number of right and appropriate answers, should be encouraged not only in the domain of art but in all disciplines. By giving consideration and support to creativity we also alter the concept of accomplishment which can no longer be narrowly measured according to a conventional yardstick, but in which originality and creative thought and activity must be recognised as factors of far greater importance.

Differentiation and individualisation

From the remarks concerning creativity it is obvious that not just one method of working (mostly that preferred by the teacher) should be employed, but that each child should find his own personal form of expression in movement. The abundant tasks that can be individually solved or that can be set by the children themselves, or by others, are helpful in this instance; in his solution each child achieves that degree of differentiation allowed by the stage he has reached in his movement development. The need to work along these lines should not mean, however, that teaching consists only of these elements. Several groups working simultaneously and collaborating on a common theme will help to develop important capacities in a child.

Training of comprehension and language development

Every discipline has its own vocabulary, the knowledge of which is necessary to the mutual understanding of certain facts. In the dance education of children aged four to ten years we are not concerned with the teaching of a terminology for dance, but with the graphic, substantial 'comprehension' and familiarity with the terms of general language and of such terms as refer to music, movement, space and time. In addition there are terms that characterise particular movements. It is important that before a term is explained, the child should have experienced the meaning of the word through his own activity. A few examples may make this clear:

jointly—individually, with each other—against each other, together—apart, simultaneously—one after the other;

above, below, in front, backwards, right, left, under, on, beside, over, through, against, high, low;

round, curved, straight, angular;

circle, arc, row, group, pair, chain;

loud, soft, heavy, light, stressed, strong;

walking, striding, strolling, sauntering, shuffling, limping, hurrying, running, swaying, pulling, pressing, striking, pushing, tapping, gliding, floating, flowing, squeezing.

Critical ability and sense of style

These two aspects pose difficult tasks for the teacher. Terms such as 'beautiful' or 'ugly' are often used subjectively and become indiscriminately fixed on traditional norms. In spite of this the children should learn to form their own judgement of a movement or a dance and should base this as much as possible on objective factors. The individual factors making up such a judgement should be known to the children through their own experiments. Teacher and pupils together should work out common standards for observation and criticism.

These include:

abundance of inspiration, assurance in performance, a capacity to enter into the spirit of the music or of the chosen text, precision in spacing and timing, lively dynamics, adaptation to partner or to the group.

It is not subjective impressions alone but their substantiation and clarification that give value to judgement and criticism. The children should make their own suggestions for improvement. For the teacher the work of training one's own movement and that of others forms the basic experience for such judgements, which incidentally, must be carefully stated, and she may never dismiss a demonstration as simply good or bad. In the discussion those points that conform to the given task have to be emphasised; apart from this the style of the performance has to be discussed. At the age of about nine or ten at the latest children are capable of the necessary detailed observation and clarity in argument.

As soon as they start dancing the dances of various periods in history in addition to their own creations and those that have been worked out by teacher and pupils together, the style of the music, of the dance steps, the ways of holding and the performance of the movements can be discussed. This, in turn, will lead gradually to a recognition of the stylistic characteristics of different periods. This can be started at primary school level in order to have a suitable basis for a more intensive study at secondary level.

Part Two
Preparing the ground for teaching

Problems of organisation

The more involved the children feel in the planning of the content and organisation of their lessons, the greater will be their interest and the more satisfactory the results. All the material and the individual examples selected must be suitable for the class in question and choice of this depends on varying factors. For details see part four, section one.

Difficulties concerning space and time and the problems of equipment are similar in nursery and primary school. It is not possible to give a general answer but some suggestions for individual solutions may be helpful.

Teaching time

In the nursery school it is advisable to combine the dance, movement and music teaching and to fit them into the daily programme in such a way that the children are occupied with these activities for a short time daily (one 20 to 25 minute period or twice 10 to 15 minutes). One might also divide the group so that some are moving while the others play or paint. Similarly in the first two years of primary school there should be a daily lesson of about 20 to 30 minutes. The ensuing result is significantly better than that which could be achieved from longer periods of time once or twice a week. Starting at about eight years old the lesson time can be increased to one hour, and two lessons a week are recommended (possibly in combination with music and physical education).

Teaching space

A frequent argument against having dance and movement education is the lack of space in the majority of schools, or the awkward layout of their rooms or construction of their buildings. This should not, however, be considered an unsurmountable obstacle. Gymnasia, recreation rooms and assembly halls, or any large class room that can be partly cleared can be used. When the teacher does not have regular use of the same room she will have to relate the subject matter of each lesson to the available space.

There are many exercises that can be performed in a classroom, even if not ideally. Tables and chairs can be placed against the walls. Such lessons should be held, if possible, at the beginning or at the end of the working day, so that only one 'rearrangement' of furniture in school hours is necessary. In time one will find the most practical solution for this reorganisation of furniture. Each child shares in the task and there is almost a competitive spirit to see who is the quietest and quickest. If a larger room suitable for movement is available, the lesson can be used to set tasks concerning the use of space, and to learn or repeat such dance forms that require a larger area. If, for reasons of organisation, one is forced to hold the classes in a small room, themes such as movement accompaniment, training of perception, exercises in co-ordination etc., are more suitable.

Ideally, the room used should have a sprung wood floor that is clean and free from splinters. Stone and concrete floors are bad for the feet and the spine. The temperature should be somewhat lower than in a classroom where the children work sitting down and keeping still. Adequate ventilation is necessary. When working in a room that is generally used for other purposes, remove all dangerous and bulky objects.

When new schools are about to be built—which is fortunately a somewhat more frequent occurrence nowadays—the teachers for music, dance and drama should help by making most precise suggestions for the layout and furnishing of the space provided for their use in order to create favourable conditions for their work.

Clothing

In general simple, light and easily washed clothing (such as tights and leotards) is recommended. In gymnasia with wooden floors gym-shoes are not necessary. Nevertheless, when the lesson is held in a classroom, or when it is not too long in duration or the physical activity not very intensive, it is enough that the children wear comfortable, loose-fitting, fairly light school clothes and soft shoes (not outdoor shoes and not slippers which give little or no support to the foot). If the teacher sometimes has to cut out the changing of clothes in order to save time, or because the lack of a suitable room for her lesson makes it unnecessary, it is obvious that she must take this into account when choosing the movement activity. The exercises should not be so strenuous that the children have to sit through the next lesson in clothes that are wet with perspiration; on the other hand the fear of excessive exertion should not limit the movements too much. The practice of not changing into special clothing should, however, be an exception, reserved for those days when dance and movement training has to take place in an ordinary classroom.

Group arrangement

Every educationalist knows that too large a group renders individual attention —especially necessary in dance education—impossible. An ideal number for dance and music groups is between 20 and 25 children in primary schools and about 15 in the nursery school. The actual situation in schools is nevertheless quite different, many classes being double these figures.

The overcrowding in our classes has a detrimental effect on children's behaviour and achievement. This fact is indisputably established through the practical experience of innumerable teachers, and emphatically confirmed by educational theorists. For the teacher who is looking for an acceptable compromise the following suggestions may be offered, even if they are not ideal:

1. The division of the class is a possibility, though not always entirely without complication. If at least one subject is taught by another teacher it may be possible to divide the class into two groups. Tuition would then be given in two different subjects by two different teachers in two different rooms. It would seem more profitable to work with full concentration once a week rather than to scrape through a senseless mass-tuition twice a week. It may even be possible to split the lesson into two half-hour sessions, one for each group, provided that two classrooms are available.

2. If the tuition can be so arranged that the dance and movement lessons come at the beginning or at the end of the school day, then it may be possible to let one group come to the lesson leaving the other group free; on another day the groups would change places.

3. For an interested group extra-curricular tuition in the form of study groups is another possibility. The great disadvantage lies in the fact that not every child can participate but only those who are specially gifted or interested.

Musical instruments

An ensemble of elemental instruments should be available with a variety of small percussion instruments (claves, tambours, tambourines, maracas, small cymbals, large cymbals, triangles, castanets, wood blocks, sleigh bells); barred percussion instruments (glockenspiels, xylophones and metallophones); bass drum and timpani, possibly some form of bass instrument and recorders.

For most schools the provision of such an ensemble of instruments is not impossible, but it is often impossible to find someone who can handle these expensive instruments. If the teacher is able to improvise on the piano for movement then a piano in the room used for movement lessons is desirable.

Other instruments that the children have learned to play can be brought in from time to time and used in the lessons.

Equipment and technical apparatus

Various items of equipment are useful for certain exercises. These include the traditional gymnastic hand equipment such as a variety of balls (small ones like tennis balls, or very large, light, inflatable plastic balls, or heavy medicine balls) ropes, hoops and canes. Hoops and canes should be available in sufficient numbers for each group and possibly in two different sizes to allow for smaller and taller children. The precise measurements can be found in sport equipment catalogues.

To the usual equipment should be added scarves, balloons, bean bags, stools, also large sheets of paper, plastic sheets, felt pens or blackboard chalks. All this equipment should be kept in suitable cupboards. After a while the children themselves should be made responsible for getting out and putting away equipment and instruments.

Besides this, record players and tape recorders are used now and then in dance lessons. There should also be facilities for showing films and slides.

Class teacher–specialist teacher–team teaching

The situation in a school in Germany is so varied that it is not stipulated who should teach dance. Ideally this should be nursery and primary school class teachers who are trained in dance, movement and music. If the qualifications and training of the class teacher are too limited, it is preferable to employ a specially trained teacher. In this case a close understanding with the class teacher should be established so that the dance and movement teacher can exploit to the full the special possibilities afforded by these lessons, e.g. in relation to the behaviour and learning capacity of the individual child.

In any case a close collaboration between all specialist teachers is desirable, especially in those spheres where subjects overlap. The music teacher, for instance, has a wider repertoire of songs and instrumental pieces at her disposal; the dance and movement teacher can help in those areas that are essentially connected with movement, like conducting, breath control in singing and the appropriate movements necessary for playing instruments.

Team teaching is also applicable to a collective performance in which music, dance and art are combined. Contrasting points of view and personal problems can greatly impede team teaching. Where it can be carried out it is undoubtedly to the advantage of every colleague. It can save much meandering and will inspire many experiments that one teacher alone might not have had the courage to attempt.

Different approaches to teaching (imitative—creative)

In the literature relating to both dance and movement education two contrasting opinions can be distinguished: the one propagates intake and assimilation directly derived through imitation, the other looks for a creative coming to grips with the subject. They can be described briefly as follows:

Imitative intake and assimilation

A technically polished exercise is demonstrated to the class by the teacher or by one of the advanced pupils and repeated by the class, with corrections from the teacher, as many times as are required for the majority of the children to master it. This, frequently called 'learning by rote' brings about the acquisition of an objective technique. Progress is faster or slower according to the different measure of skill and capacity for concentration of each child; that means that one group is mostly underchallenged, while another, less skilled, is over-challenged. With this method it is impossible to reach the individual ability of each child. The children's imagination and capacity for expression are hardly touched.

The acquisition of certain, mostly superficially imitated movements and dance steps predominates and often becomes an end in itself. Only too often concern for the suitability of the work for the child, clarity, spontaneity, personalisation and other basic considerations of modern educational thought are neglected. When the apparent results are more important to the teacher (and to his employers) than is the development of the child's personal abilities (other than in imitation) then the very purpose of teaching is lost.

Creative ways of working

The material that is to be covered is organised by the teacher and divided into various working stages. Out of the material of the individual stages the children are given suitable tasks according to their abilities, and through the tackling and solving of them they gain technical skill as well as spatial, dynamic and rhythmic experiences.

The tasks can be arranged in such a way as to place the main emphasis on rhythmic variations, working with a partner, musical accompaniment, or on spatial experiments, technical difficulties, group formations or ways of holding. Some tasks are worked out by individual children, others by groups of different sizes. The essential point is that the children are not given a model to imitate, but that they should reach a solution through their own attempts and ideas. Increased experience, encouragement derived from the success of others and increased self-confidence gained from their own successes will lead to even better results. As soon as some basic experience has been acquired, the children themselves will be able to provide ideas for further tasks.

Difficulties and dangers can also follow from this way of working. The teacher has to observe the children in a far more differentiated way. It is no longer the class as a whole that is her partner, but each individual child. More time is generally required to achieve 'results' through this creative way of working than through the imitative one. Nevertheless, by setting the children individual tasks every gift can be furthered, so that time lost by over or under challenging can be used to better purpose.

Another danger may lie in the possibility that each child may become fixed exclusively in his own personal movement style. Through careful observation and compensatory exercises this can nevertheless be avoided. Naturally the individual style of each child will be reasonably pronounced, but this will be his own, personal, characteristic style of movement and not that of the teacher as imitated by the whole class.

Comparison of the two methods

Imitative, deductive, direct	*Creative, inductive, indirect*
Standardised execution of movement, objective technique	Individual exploration, discovery and execution of movement, subjective technique
Danger of superficial imitation without personal inner experience. Importance of achievement	Danger of a lack of form (without a common form comparisons are more difficult), process of experience important
Basic material produces objective material for exercises. Direction, demonstration and imitation, correction from the teacher	Material dependent upon children concerned. Movement theme— individual solutions, self-selected tasks
Normal disciplinary difficulties with simultaneous and uniform execution of movements	More discipline problems through greater freedom of performance in time and space
Time-saving—economic—objective	Results take up more time, consideration of individual
Through giving same tasks to everyone less gifted are overtaxed, more gifted undertaxed	The setting of individual tasks makes for optimal furthering of individual needs

Subordination, accommodation, "working to order" are demanded	Self-reliance, coequality, responsibility for self are developed
Powers of observation and imitation are developed	Imagination and creative attitudes are stimulated
Teacher centred through announcement, control, criticism	Child centred, teacher assumes more self-effacing role as initiator and helper
Convergent thinking is encouraged	Divergent thinking is encouraged

Combination of both ways of working

The purpose of dance education is not just to impart technique and teach some fixed dance forms, nor is it, by contrast, to let the children play as a kind of therapy through activity; on the contrary, it is important that the children learn to move and to express themselves through dance. This capacity will be developed through short improvisations, group dancing of an elemental or folk character, through presenting fairy tales or other short scenes in dance. For adolescents contemporary or historical social dances and abstract dance themes can be added. These may often be connected with school plays.

To attain this end the initial spontaneity needs to be sustained, and the imagination and the desire to experiment needs to be stimulated. Only in this way can the children achieve their own results and largely avoid imitating the teacher. The most logical initial step towards this achievement is the provision of individually designed tasks. Reassurance and appreciation are important, even in the simplest tasks, for they give self-confidence and encouragement for tackling new and more difficult assignments. The children do not only learn through overcoming their own difficulties but also through observing others. Various different solutions should therefore often be demonstrated by individuals or groups. The resulting observations can then be briefly discussed.

On the other hand, after an appropriate period of time, the children in a class or group should also, as far as possible, have evolved a common, objective, technical grounding. It is at the age of 8 to 10 years that the most favourable psychological and physical conditions exist for well-balanced, intensive work at basic forms of movement, their variations and combinations. Individual experiments and demonstrations are also included at this stage. After observing and comparing individual solutions (but not before the age of 7-8 years) some elements can be selected and practised, or examples that the children themselves consider successful can be tried out by all those who have seen them. At the stage when the teacher makes corrections or points out possibilities that have not been fully exploited, she should help and stimulate through her own demonstration.

In teaching, creative and imitative work do not entirely exclude each other, but it is essential to consider carefully by which means particular elements and aims can best be achieved.

43

Every teacher knows that for the planning of lessons and the development of more complex movement themes there is no generally valid system. The teacher's preparation must be so flexible that his intended plan can allow for the kinetic and psychological situation of the group concerned, can incorporate the ideas and suggestions given by the children and can, under certain circumstances, be radically changed. The ability of the teacher to be flexible and spontaneous is of tremendous importance and this facility should be trained.

Nevertheless, with reference to the new psychology of learning it is possible to outline stages that will show the process by which a theme is worked out, each stage having to correspond to the material concerned.

1) Motivation—Exploration
2) 1. Activity—Experiment
3) Reflection—Choice
4) 2. Activity—Execution
5) Reflection—Recapitulation

1) At this stage the interest for the new theme is awakened, the appropriate atmosphere is introduced and established and the theme, together with all the general problems that it presents, is defined.

2) The first activity stage should yield sufficient opportunity for the children to come to terms with the problem, to tackle it from different angles and to gain their own experiences· of it. Subjective knowledge is made possible as the individual comes to terms with the new material.

3) The experiment is resolved through a phase of reflection in which that which has been tried out is considered. Different starting points are shown and discussed. The wide range of possibilities is reduced with regard to the original problem—in some cases with relation to the new experiences gained in 2). A selection of the most suitable suggestions is decided upon and a plan is made for working these out in terms of technique and form.

4) At this second activity stage the actual working out and clear defining of the previous ideas and experiments takes place. The emphasis can be placed on technical or compositional elements. One is striving for the best realisation attainable.

5) In the last and concluding period of reflection the results should be shown again and considered. In the several versions differences and common factors should be established, suggestions for improvement and for possible development or variation should be made. As long as they can be verbalised, fresh experiences can be formulated and new concepts defined. Connections with already known, free associations should be suggested.

Combination with other subject areas

In an earlier chapter the establishment of the relationship between dance, movement, music and language was attempted. There it was seen that these individual elements overlap and influence each other. This overlap will be briefly further outlined, with some suggestions.

Music

The teaching of music and dance or movement should be interlinked as much as possible. In Orff-Schulwerk and in Eurhythmics we find the fundamental concept that music and movement are inseparable in an elemental education. A wealth of models and, furthermore, a methodical approach to fundamental music and dance education are to be found in the examples of Orff-Schulwerk, and in other collections based mainly upon it.

Elements of music and dance are closely related: tempo, rhythm, dynamics, various metres and fundamental forms can be approached from either discipline. The beginnings of musical notation (pre-notation) and conducting, or the less demanding beating of time, can be prepared in the movement lesson. In addition it is possible to show different styles, such as those relating to folklore and early court dances through the medium of dance and music respectively. This assignment should certainly be started at the age of nine or ten so that the involvement with such problems can be based upon it when they reach the secondary stage of education. Songs and instrumental pieces with a strong motoric character stimulate expression in movement. Conversely, dance forms, combinations of movements or other short movement motifs give ideas and stimulation for musical improvisation while the movement accompaniment, performed by the children themselves, develops perception of dynamics, rhythm and form. The children, with the help of their teacher, can compose and play their own music for exercises as well as for short, fixed dance pieces.

A series of examples for the practical application of the principles described above will be given in subsequent chapters. The musical aspect, as it occurs in these examples, will be considered as far as it is relevant to this book.

Language—Literature

Rhymes, proverbs, verses and songs have always been part of children's play and dance. Often their meaning, when descriptive or dramatic, but frequently also the sound or rhythm of the spoken word offers a stimulus for dance. Any

45

selection must naturally be made from particular considerations. For the age group under consideration here counting-out rhymes, riddles, sayings, nursery rhymes, together with proverbs, fairy tales and fables are suitable. Apart from the use made of these literary miniatures, movement education can also help with language training. This has already been touched upon on p. 32.

Drawing—Painting—Craftwork

Line, shape and form are terms common to the plastic and graphic arts as well as to dance. The more experience that children acquire in relation to both these forms of expression, the more clearly they will be able to express themselves in their childlike creations, and the better they will later understand works of art in architecture, sculpture, painting, graphic and ornamental art.

Some specific tasks lead, for instance, to discovering and trying out variously shaped paths across the room. From this spirals, meandering shapes, angles and curves are formed. These patterns are walked or traversed in some other way singly, in pairs, in small groups, in chains or in rows. They can be drawn on the floor, in the air, on the blackboard or on large sheets of paper and with different kinds of material. The children can also consider where else such figures can be found. Observations can be discussed, photographs and pictures examined and some of the shapes seen can be fed back into movement.

Abstract terms like repetition, contrast, contrary motion and variation belong to music, to dance and to the fine arts. They can become a concrete experience through movement.

Flowing, sustained arm and hand movements, the drawing of design-based and melodic shapes in the air and on the floor are preparatory exercises that can benefit both writing and musical notation.

With simple sketches the children can also try to record some small dance pieces. Such rudiments of dance notation are possible as soon as the individual symbols are understood. The content of songs and of danced texts inspire drawing and painting and also sculpture. Costumes and scenery, not only for performances but also for the purpose of classwork, can be designed and made by the children with the teacher's help.

Part Three
Material for Dance Education

Explanation of notation*

right hand or right foot: note stem up

left hand or left foot: note stem down

both hands or both feet: note stems up and down

one foot closes to the other
without transfer of weight: note in brackets   (♩) (♩)

stamp

take off

striking feet together in the air

change step   CS

scissors jump   SJ

stamp without transfer of weight

front facing the movement direction--forwards

back facing the movement direction--backwards

right shoulder facing the movement direction--
               sideways to the right

left shoulder facing the movement direction--
               sideways to the left

continuous movement in one direction   or
            e.g. walking   walking   running

continuous movement with change of direction

movement on the spot   Spt.

whole turn

half turn

quarter turn

finger-snapping	Sn.	stamping	St.
clapping	Cl.	speaking	Sp.
thigh-slapping (Patschen)	Pa.	step	Stp.

* see also glossary on page 211.

Preparatory exercises for
relaxed movement and music-making

A posture that is free from tension is a necessary prerequisite for flowing harmonious movement, for playing an instrument without tension, for the production of a good tone in speaking, singing and recorder playing, and for conducting and beating time.

Even the teacher who has no specialist movement training has to be able to teach movement progressively and to recognise and correct faulty posture. For this reason there follows a selection of games and exercises of a type that is indispensable if the tuition is to be something more than merely keeping the children occupied. It is true that very young children do not yet need any specific physical training but the teacher needs help in approaching the checking of a faulty posture and encouraging a good one. The younger the children are the more these exercises should seem like games.

Some of the following examples (especially those concerning relaxation and posture) should be used in varied ways for a short time in each lesson. The choice of material depends upon the requirements of the children.

Games and exercises for
warming-up at the beginning of a lesson

The so-called "warming-up exercises" have several aims. First, the initial hunger for movement, the spontaneous need to run and romp about the room, must be satisfied. Once this surplus of accumulated energy has been discharged, the interest in and the ability to concentrate on quieter and more clearly defined activities will become significantly greater. Apart from this the purpose is to warm up the muscles. This occurs through movements that stimulate breathing and blood circulation. Such exercises become absolutely essential in winter and after having spent a long time sitting down in school. The sudden exercising of cold muscles can lead to injury. This is less likely to occur with small children than with adolescents and adults.

Locomotion exercises

—Children warm up quickly with catching games and find them specially enjoyable. One rule must be observed: no bumping either against the wall or into another child. Variations: everyone moves on all fours (both hands must

touch the floor, the "catcher" may of course have one hand free to catch).
—The teacher gives the tempo with a drum and the children take it up. They can alternate in running, skipping, and—as a rest—walking. This can be done freely round the room or in a group, in which case the teacher should see that the leader is changed as often as possible.
—The children run. At a predetermined signal from the teacher (a call, an accented drum beat, the accompaniment stops) the children gather together in a corner or by the blackboard, by the window, in the middle of the room or in a circle round the teacher. The specified place must be reached as quickly as possible.
—The children run or skip. At a call from the teacher each child should see how quickly he can get into any one of the following positions: lying down on stomach or back, squatting, sitting cross-legged, sitting on the heels or sitting with legs together and straight.

Different ways of sitting: knees bent double and legs to one side; legs apart and straight; arms clasping bent knees: on the heels; legs together and straight; cross-legged.

From running freely round the room, at a call from the teacher, the children should form a circle, a chain, pairs, a line or two concentric circles as quickly as possible. (Here reaction exercises are combined with orientation to the room and space-awareness.) Suggestions for various room formations can be found on pp. 68-70.

Exercises on the spot

—The children stand, well spaced out so that each has enough room. They stretch, making themselves "wide" and contract making themselves "narrow", at first slowly, then gradually getting faster.
—The same can be done while lying on the floor. In this case the movement can lead from lying on the back to a sitting position, or from lying on the back to lying on the stomach or the side.
—Each child can experiment with the ways in which he can move hands, elbows, the whole arm, the shoulders. Bending and stretching, turning inwards and outwards, circling and shaking are all possible. The children should be reminded that they can vary both the speed and the amount of energy used.

Exercises for loosening-up and removing tension

Many adults, and all too often children are excessively cramped and tense. While working at a music or movement task one can see that the natural ability to relax out of undue tension has disappeared. Many find themselves in a state of perpetual tension. This is reflected in tense features, shoulders held high, stiff arms and legs, irregular and shallow breathing and an excessive use of energy for even the smallest movement. The results of these faults are: premature tiredness, movement and music-making which is unrhythmic and therefore imprecise, uncertainty and exaggerated intensity of tone in speaking, singing and recorder playing, excessive muscle contraction resulting in ugly, unharmonious movement. These tensions often have a psychological as well as a physical reason. Only in rare cases will it be possible for the teacher to discover these reasons during the lesson. The opportunity of talking to colleagues or to the child's parents outside school hours may present itself, however, and lead to the discovery of the cause. The teacher can nevertheless do a little to help shy and anxious children overcome their inhibitions and tension through providing a friendly and calm atmosphere during the lesson.

Loosening-up and relaxation exercises should not be continued for too long, but they should be specially introduced if tension arises. By this means the children will understand why these exercises are done and will recognise their effect. They should really be able to feel for themselves, and learn through watching others, whether a movement is executed with too much, too little, or with the right amount of energy.

Relaxation exercises

--After strenuous exercises the children lie on their backs and close their eyes. This automatically regulates the breathing (1, 2, 3).*
--The children lie on the floor. The teacher goes from one to the other and raises an arm or a leg and lowers it again carefully. If tension is present the arm or leg will remain "standing-up" in the air, if it is relaxed it will immediately fall through the force of gravity (1, 2, 3).
--The children lie on their stomachs. The teacher takes hold of them at the waist and lifts them up. The upper part of the trunk, the head and limbs should hang down limply. This can also be done when the children are lying on their backs (2, 3).
--From the basic, standing stretching-up position the children drop into a crouching position, letting the movement come to stillness naturally with small bouncing movements and then slowly straighten up again. The breath should not be held. As a general rule breathing out coincides with relaxation, breathing

---

*The numbers in brackets refer to the different age levels, details of which are given on pp. 149–151.

in with straightening up. Humming or whispering a consonant (s, pf, f) helps to control it (3).

Total relaxation–
the teacher helps

—For younger children, falling exercises can be associated with a number of images (the melting of a snowman, a tree being blown down by the wind). The children usually become so engrossed with their game that falling does not frighten them. Should it be otherwise, however, a mat can be put on the floor (1, 2, 3).

—Playing marionettes: it will be best if the teacher can bring a hand puppet or marionette to the lesson and show what happens to a puppet when the string is slackened: the respective part of the body falls down.

Playing marionettes: partial, progressive relaxation

53

The children try this now with their own bodies. Thus they learn as part of a game to relax one part of the body after the other. They should feel the weight of their limbs. First the hands fall, then the arms, the head, the trunk, until the whole body sinks to the ground. (Anxious children can try this out on the mat). (2, 3).

Loosening-up exercises

Active loosening-up exercises are those in which a part of the body is loosened by shaking or swinging it.

--Head: let it fall forwards onto the chest, or sideways, or backwards into the nape of the neck. Turn the head from side to side, shake it and nod, but not too fast (1, 2, 3).

--Shoulders: "shrug" the shoulders, raise them and let them fall, rotate them both forwards and backwards, later in contrary motion (2, 3).

--Trunk: practise quick stretching and collapsing in turn (2, 3). With legs apart and from a sitting or standing position let the upper part of the trunk fall forward, a slight wave-like undulating movement flows through the upper trunk and the hanging limbs respond gently with small, bouncing movements (head, neck and arms are relaxed) (3).

--Hands: shake both hands in all directions (palms facing towards each other, towards the face, away from the body). Ideas to help the imagination: sprinkle oneself with water, shake the drops off the fingers, play the piano in the air (1, 2, 3).

--Arms: very loose, "floppy" clapping in front, above, behind or to the side (1, 2, 3). Bounce the elbows up and down, keeping the hands still in front of the chest (the hands are at first held by another child, later the fingers are loosely entwined or the hands remain "stationary" by themselves) (3). Hands remaining near the thighs, elbows bounce outwards away from the body (2, 3).

--Legs: Using alternate legs shake or swing them in front, to the side or behind (1, 2, 3). Swinging one leg from front to back, and from far to near the body (2, 3). Lying on the back, lift the legs to a vertical position and kick into the air with them, and shake them. Relax the legs, the knees bending and sinking onto the chest (2, 3).

--Feet: sitting on the floor with knees bent up, alternately shake right then left foot (1, 2, 3), tap lightly on the floor with the ball of the foot (2, 3).

Passive loosening-up exercises are most effective when they are performed lying down with the eyes closed. In this position all unnecessary tensions are avoided and passivity is assisted. The part of the body to be relaxed should rarely be touched by one's own hand, but slightly shaken by the teacher or by one's partner.

--Lying on the stomach: the partner takes hold of the ankles of the prone child and shakes them carefully in all directions. The muscles of the leg and foot are thus thoroughly loosened (1, 2, 3).

--Now the leg, bent at the knee, is held by the ankle bone and shaken sideways to and fro with short, sharp movements. The partner should preferably kneel by the feet of the prone child. With this exercise a loosening of the muscles of the lower leg will be achieved (2, 3).

Using this shaking action all the limbs can be loosened as follows:

—Lying on the back: holding the forearm near the wrist loosens the hands. Holding the hand near the wrist loosens the whole arm up to the shoulders (1, 2, 3).

—Holding the foot by the ankle, loosens the muscles of the legs and buttocks (1, 2, 3).

Passive loosening of hands and feet — with help from a partner

Passive relaxation without the help of a partner produces a more limited result, for the hand that does the shaking becomes very tired.

Tension exercises

Tension and the exertion of energy in various degrees are necessary in both movement and music. Such exercises should nevertheless be practised with care. The teacher must be able to recognise which children have less muscular strength; here tension exercises are appropriate. Over-tense children should rarely be given the following exercises and their variations, and then only in limited measure. Before one can consciously tense the body one has to learn how to use its energies properly. This is at first best done against something that offers resistance (wall, floor or partner). First the energy of the whole body is employed because this gives the clearest experience. Later varying degrees of energy can be applied to moving different parts of the body.

Exercises demanding the use of energy

A child sits on the floor: another tries to lift him up (1, 2, 3). (Child doing the lifting: energy; seated child: energy and weight.)
—Two children stand back to back and each tries to push the other away; they are here pushing against the floor as well as against their partner's body (1, 2, 3).
—A child stands with feet well apart and firmly planted on the floor; his partner tries to dislodge him (1, 2, 3).
—Tug-of-war and similar games belong to this category.
—Later one tries to localise the use of energy by letting the child pull with one hand or be pulled away by one leg, for instance (1, 2, 3).

Tension exercises for the whole body in game form

—A child stands between two other children and makes himself quite stiff. The other children push him gently and carefully to and fro. This game, under various names and sometimes called "rocking the dummy", is very popular among children and widely played (3).

Total tension with the help of partners

—The children lie on the floor, stiff as felled trees. The teacher lifts one arm, then one leg to see whether it really is as stiff as a branch. She can also raise the whole "tree" by lifting the child from below the shoulders. Arms, head and legs should not hang down and the pelvis should not sag (2, 3). (Opposite exercise: p. 52.)

—"Casting and uncasting spells": this is taken from a children's game that offers a good stimulus for work in muscular tension but also for alternating between relaxation and tension. It is known under various names including "Petrified" and "Statues". One child plays the sorcerer; any child he touches becomes rigid — like a statue — in any position according to choice. When released by being touched by another, not yet bewitched, child, he is free to run about the room once more.

Tension exercises "bewitched"

That then is the game. It can be slightly altered to fit our purpose. At a given acoustic signal (the sound of a cymbal, a magic word, etc.) all children stop dead in their tracks adopting some posture; they mostly choose very strange and grotesque positions. The sorcerer now goes round and gently touches the statues to see whether they are really made of stone or whether they move at the slightest touch. The release from the spell (again an acoustic signal) can be total or partial; the arms alone could first be released, for instance, then the head and then the hands, and so on until in the end the 'statues' have become children again (2, 3).

Partial tension exercises

While doing the following exercises the teacher must take every care that no stiffness in any other part of the body (neck, face, hands) arises.
—While in the act of swinging an arm or loosely shaking a leg these are stiffened either in the fully stretched or in the tightly bent positions (2, 3).
—Sitting with legs together and straight: alternation of tension and relaxation of the leg and pelvis muscles. As the muscles are stiffened one can clearly see the body rising slightly, and as they relax it falls back again (2, 3).
—Lying on the back: while shaking and waving arms and legs (like a beetle on its back) at a signal the children suddenly stiffen one arm or one leg, at another time both arms or both legs, later the left arm and the right leg, for instance. For this, however, quite an amount of training in co-ordination is necessary (3).

57

Posture exercises

Good posture, as we term it, is the upright position that is functionally correct in standing, sitting and in locomotion. There is undoubtedly a considerable reciprocal relationship between the internal attitude and the external carriage of a human being. Each inner emotion has its own influence on the external bearing and, equally, the education of the external bearing can influence the psychological attitude. Through experience and observation children learn what a good, lifted posture in standing looks like; each joint should stand above the other, i.e. the knee-joint above the foot-joint, above it the hip-joint, above the pelvis girdle the shoulder belt, neck and head lifted, the crown of the head (not the nose) upwards towards the ceiling.

In time the children learn to note their own and others' faults in posture. The teacher should set an example with her own posture and, when necessary, help by correcting the children.

General posture exercises

--For standing and walking: to strengthen the feeling of the upright position use objects that the children can carry on their heads (small beanbags, hand drums, articles of clothing, books). This is first tried out while standing, then while walking forwards and backwards, finally the children turn or kneel down on one knee. The hands may only come to the rescue at the beginning (1, 2, 3). The same can be done with imaginary objects (e.g. walking with a crown or a jug on one's head (1, 2, 3).

--Stretching and sitting up straight (legs straight out in front or cross-legged): alternate stretching up and sinking down (let the imagination help by thinking of puppet strings alternately pulled and released). The stretching is intensified if the arms are taken high above the head (2, 3).

--Stretching while lying down: the children lie on their backs with arms stretched out above their heads. From this stretched position they should roll onto their stomachs, and the reverse, until finally they roll on their own axis round the room (1, 2, 3).

--A child and the teacher hold a rope so that it is suspended just over the heads of the children who pass underneath it (lower it a little for small children, raise it for taller ones). If they stretch well enough they should be able to reach the rope with their heads (1, 2, 3).

--Exercises with a cane, a ball, or with a rope held tautly between the hands will give further stimuli.

--Wriggling like a snake on the floor, either on the back or on the stomach, increases the necessary mobility of the spine. Wriggling around obstacles (1, 2).

The two most common posture defects are a hollow back and round shoulders. In severe cases the teacher should recommend orthopaedic gymnastics, since the short time available, as well as the fact that class work is done in groups, leaves insufficient time for the individual postural attention necessary for such a child. Some basic exercises for all children should however be mentioned.

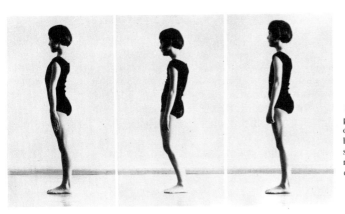

Extreme defects of posture: overtension and hollow back; sloppy posture and round shoulders; correct posture.

Exercises to correct hollow back

Basically all exercises that make the back round are helpful, and all those which lead to excessive arching of the back are dangerous:

--Bounce up and down in squatting position: keeping the arms round the knees roll backwards onto heels and then rock forwards and backwards (2, 3).

--Lie on the back, the legs drawn up, the soles of the feet and the small of the back remaining on the floor: the legs are slowly stretched as far as they can be without letting the small of the back leave the floor (3).

--Stand against the wall with heels almost touching it: press the small of the back against the wall (3).

Variation 1: Begin curling the spine head first down on the chest, then the shoulders and upper back but keeping the small of the back pressed against the wall (2,3).

Variation 2: Press the whole spine against the wall, then, bending the knees, slide the body down the wall till the squatting position is reached (2, 3).

The next two exercises will make the children recognise the difference between a straight back, a hollow back, and round shoulders:

--Lie on the back, the legs drawn up, soles of the feet on the floor: raise the small of the back high enough to be able to slide a hand between spine and floor (like a ship passing under a bridge). The small of the back is then pressed against the floor (the bridge is lowered, no ship can pass through) (1, 2, 3).

--Kneel on all fours: the teacher places her hand on the small of the child's back, he pushes this hand up and away (the spine is curved by this action) then lets it sink slowly down into the hollow back position (without any pressure from the teacher's assisting hand), finally pressing the hand up again ending with the spine straight (2, 3).

59

Exercises to correct round shoulders

Exercises that lead to the mobility and stretching of the spine in the region of the dorsal vertebrae are helpful.

—Kneel on all fours: relaxing the elbows press the breastbone down towards the floor and gently bounce the trunk up and down in this position, also move along the floor in this position (2, 3).

—Lie on the stomach: move along the floor with and without the help of the hands (1, 2, 3).

—Lie on the stomach, arms stretched over the head: raise the arms and chest from the floor and relax; then the legs—knees straight; then both simultaneously—rock to and fro in this position (imagining a rocking horse) (3).

—Two children sit back to back, arms stretched upwards and holding hands: one at a time each child tries to pull the other over his back, thus the spine of the passive child is arched backwards (3).

—Bend and stretch while sitting cross-legged or with the legs stretched out in front, with hands clasped behind the neck (3).

Strengthening exercises

When many different movements are practised, and especially if this practice is frequent and intensive, the child's body must be sufficiently prepared, otherwise it will be overtaxed resulting in faulty posture and damage. It seems therefore appropriate to describe here a short selection of exercises that are intended to strengthen the body.

Exercises to strengthen feet and legs

Good grip with the toes, ability to adapt to the floor surface, soft, rolling action of the feet and the development of increased elasticity in the ankle joints are essential prerequisites for effective locomotion. Exercises to this end should be practised without footwear.

—Various exercises of gripping the floor: picking up small objects with the toes (handkerchiefs, pencils, small balls, drumsticks), tearing paper, picking up the torn pieces from the floor and carrying them about (1, 2, 3).

—Adapting the feet to various surfaces: walking on grass, polished floor, carpet, walking on a rope with the toes curled round it (1, 2, 3).

—To make the toes mobile: bend them up and down, spread them out. These exercises can be practised simultaneously with hands and feet. Whether standing up or sitting down the upright position of the trunk must be noted. A friendly glance from the teacher will suffice to remind the children of this.

—Bend and stretch the feet when they are not bearing weight. Rotate them in in both directions (2, 3).

both feet, heels just off the floor, bounce up and down, later
/, one foot at a time. One can change every time between right and
) or bounce on each foot twice, three times, or more often before
3).
while in the squatting position without using the hands will
all the muscles of the legs (1, 2, 3).
sit back on the heels: bounce up and down. Imagine riding a horse
1s the thigh and pelvis muscles) (2).
elastic repulsion of one foot from the floor, drawing the knee right
chest, the supporting leg straight and slightly turned out (also to be
/ith a slight outward turning of the trunk) (3).

strengthen the trunk

rcises strengthen partly the stomach and partly the back muscles.
ees drawn up to the chest, soles of the feet on the floor: straighten
ront and draw them up again. Repeat slowly at first, then increasing
Change also from sitting with legs stretched wide to knees drawn up
(2, 3).
back: bring knees up onto the chest keeping the small of the back
e floor (control this with one hand, there should be no room for
spine and floor): stretch the legs out slowly one at a time just above
it only so far as is possible without allowing the small of the back
, 3).
back, arms stretched out above the head: contract quickly into a
ting position, arms round knees, head on knees, uncurl slowly to
position. Lying on the side, stretch and curl up alternately (2, 3).
—S   uickly raise one knee and clasp both arms around it; change
quickly from one leg to the other (2, 3).

By using balls and canes one can modify similar exercises and bring a greater
variety to them.
—Lying on the stomach: lift trunk and legs alternately or simultaneously (as
described under exercises to correct round shoulders) (3).
—Sitting cross-legged or with the legs spread wide: bend trunk forwards and press
into the floor with small bouncing movements, then stretch the back with small
bouncing movements (3).
—Stand with legs apart: relax upper trunk downwards, first straighten the back
(parallel to the floor) and then come to standing (3).
—Sit on the heels which are held by hands throughout: push the pelvis upwards
and forwards till the groin is stretched. To offset this round the back again at
once and bend forward touching the floor with the forehead (3).

Exercises for use
between sessions of instrumental playing

Tiredness, inattentiveness, and tension in the shoulder, arm and back muscles will arise after long periods of sitting at instruments or of concentrated music writing. In such cases an interval of two minutes for physical and mental relaxation is far more helpful than any exhortation on the part of the teacher. Yawning and general lack of attention show a slackening of the capacity for concentration, not necessarily a lack of interest.

—Beaters, pencils and ballpoint pens are laid aside, still sitting, the children relaxing entirely, sink down till their chests lie on their thighs and their arms hang down to the floor.

—The children stand up, noiselessly placing the stools slightly to the back so that the instruments are out of danger. They shake hands and arms, raise them up in the air and loosely let them fall again, giving at the knees. They repeat this several times. At the last time they drop right down to a squatting position allowing the downward impulse to fade out with a few small bouncing movements.

—Standing with feet together the arms are flung round the body from one side to the other while allowing the knees to give naturally (there must be enough room between the children). The movement is large at first and gradually becomes smaller.

—Nod extremely slowly so that the head falls first backwards onto the nape of the neck and then onto the chest (make sure it falls loosely). Also slowly turn the head so that the chin arrives first over the right and then over the left shoulder. Then swing the head briskly from side to side, lastly, describe a circle with it.

—Interlace the fingers of both hands in front of the body, press the palms up to the ceiling; the body bends slightly backwards, the head falls back onto the nape of the neck.

—Now the fingers are interlaced behind the body, the outsides of the hands pulled right back so that the shoulder blades are drawn together. When the hands are pressed towards the ceiling the body bends forwards.

—Lastly, the children run around their own stools and then freely round the room, in a chain, in a group behind a leader (skipping is also possible). At a signal from the teacher they step quickly and quietly up onto their stools (that must of course be incapable of falling or slipping) and then they jump down noiselessly.

Such exercises, or others that are similar, should not be thought of as 'training'; they should provide fun for the children. They can be replaced by others that, while partly prescribed, leave room for individual solutions.

—The children should stretch and reach out, and yawn if they want to; then suddenly sit on the floor and toss their hands and feet in the air, letting them 'fly'; from sitting they change to lying down and then to standing again, always trying to find new ways of changing from one position to the other.

—Lastly, the children sit on their stools again, shut their eyes and sway the upper part of their bodies from side to side with movements that always become smaller and smaller until they cease, with the body in the upright position.

Now, instrumental playing, rhythmic exercises, singing or writing can start again; tiredness is over for a while and the children can concentrate once more.

Preparatory exercises for conducting

Simple songs and instrumental pieces can soon be conducted by the children themselves. Naturally one cannot expect them to lead a group through dynamic and rhythmic phrasing, nor in the musical interpretation of a piece. With the help of simple patterns of beating that are prepared by patschen, clapping, and snapping the fingers, they learn to beat the different units of time (two-four, three-four and four-four and later five-or seven-four). Beginnings and endings must be clearly conveyed. When a child undertakes the role of 'conductor' he will immediately have a feeling of responsibility towards the group as well as towards the song or instrumental piece that he wants to conduct.

Through the following exercises a certain sensitivity of arm movements (dabbing, elastic and sustained movements) should be achieved and the various beating patterns learned.

—The teacher plays a short, rhythmic phrase that is repeated several times (hand drum, clapping, claves). The children sketch out the main accents in the air (they can pretend they hold a paint brush in each hand dabbing blobs of paint in the air in as many directions as possible). This gives them an elastic, precise hand movement that is later indispensable to conducting, and which is practised in advance in a playful and imaginative way. This and the following exercise can at first actually be done with brush and paint, though the movements should be performed later without paper and paint.

—The teacher now plays a legato melody on a recorder; if no instrument is available the melody can be sung. The shape of the melody is painted by the children in the air, first with one hand, then the other and finally with both hands. Through this imitative drawing of melodic shapes flowing arm movements should be achieved.

—Practising giving an entry: this may at first be exaggerated and crude, as though the children wanted to pick something up and throw it on the floor, or, if they are sitting, as if they wanted to strike the floor with their fist. They must ensure that the up-beat movement coincides with breathing in, the down-beat with breathing out. The breathing in should not be slower than the down-beat. A good example from the teacher will be a great help. Later on these movements should become smaller and more precise.

—Two-four time: the beating pattern of two-four time arises out of alternate patschen and finger-snapping. After the patschen on the accented down-beat the hands rebound from the thigh up to the finger-snapping (unaccented beat).

63

Finger
Snapping.
Patschen.

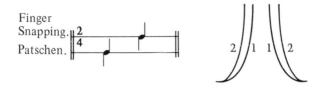

—Three-four time; bouncy patschen on the thigh on one, to finger-snapping in an outward direction on two, then above the head and another finger-snap on three.

Snapping.
Patschen.

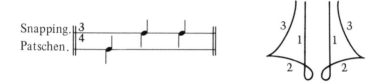

—Four-four time: patschen for the accented beat, on two the hands are brought together in clapping, on three hand and arm movement in an outwards direction (finger-snap), on four the arms are raised to another finger snap.

Snapping.
Clapping.
Patschen.

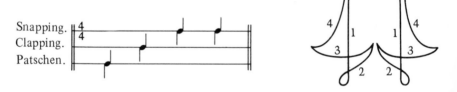

The teacher should see that all these exercises are performed without tension (see relaxation and loosening-up exercises).

This 'beating time' is of course not practised abstractly, but is occasionally used as a rhythmic accompaniment to songs, sayings or rhymes.

—The children sit in a semicircle and recite a short verse in two-four time, and to this they use the appropriate rhythmic accompaniment using sound gestures, given above. One child sits in front of the group in the place of the teacher, gives the entry and tries, after a while to leave out the acoustic representation of the beats until he is, in fact, conducting in two-four time.

—For another text or another song (this time in three-four time) the change-over from audible to inaudible representation of the beats is tried out, that is, once with sound gestures and once without.

As soon as the sounds are omitted the arm movements are reduced. Every unnecessary gesticulation with arms and hands is to be avoided. After a while these conducting movements should be related to the dynamics of the piece concerned by becoming smaller or larger, but in every case they should be clear and precise.

Preparation for conducting through sound gestures: four-four time

—The children stand in two groups opposite one another; the teacher plays a melody on a recorder. Through a sign she indicates which group should conduct to it. A change-over occurs always at the end of a phrase. In doing so it is a good idea to vary the tempo (though the change-over should occur very smoothly) and the children try to listen and to match their movements to the speed taken by the teacher (or child in her place).

Once the children are secure in their performance of two-four and three-four time, and when they understand the accentual structure of these times (this does not mean that they are secure in the corresponding notation), then two-four and three-four can be combined.

—One group (possibly girls only) speaks a verse or a sequence of names in three-four time:

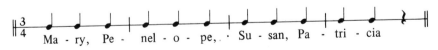

Ma - ry, Pe - nel - o - pe, · Su - san, Pa - tri - cia

Then the second group (boys only or children with low pitched voices) comes in with a name sequence or a verse in two-four time.

At first the group concerned speak their text twice in combination with audible conducting movements (using sound gestures). Then the words are mouthed silently and as silently conducted.

--A melody to these words can be found; one group sings, the other conducts, later they change places.

--The teacher plays, and repeats several times, a short melody that contains a change of time. The children clap to it at first and then try to conduct it. Then the rhythm only can be notated and finally the pitch added.

--The children should be given the task of finding two or three songs at home, and of preparing them for singing to their own conducting. If possible each song should be in a different time.

--One child starts to sing a well-known melody, the other children join in and conduct; the teacher or one of the children conducts in a certain tempo, perhaps in three-four time, and each child should think of a well-known melody that fits, or improvise one.

--Change between 'loud' and 'soft': two groups sit opposite one another, the first group sings or speaks a text that the second group repeats softly. The children accompany their singing by conducting, with large movements when loud and small movements when soft. Then one child starts them off, and, according to his movements the other children sing or speak loudly or softly.

It is sensible to allow children to conduct in front of a group as often as possible. Every song and every instrumental piece that is currently being worked at can, when repeated, be conducted by another child in the group. Conducting encourages self-reliance and discipline. When a child notices how difficult it is to start when individual children are inattentive, he will be more likely to behave in the group in a more concentrated way.

The space, time and dynamic aspects
of movement performance

Every movement takes place in space. It requires a certain time, governed by the rhythm of the activity, and is inseparably concerned with dynamics, that is with the input of energy from which the movement arises. Space, time and dynamics then, determine the kind of movement. In a survey the most important variations of such a realisation should be presented. It is a concentrated summary of those applications that cccur in the countless small examples of daily teaching.

Space

In describing the spatial aspects of movement the following have to be distinguished:
Direction: There are six main movement directions: forwards–backwards, upwards–downwards, side to side, diagonals (they have no great significance at the beginning of dance education) and turning, inwards and outwards.
Dimension: far–near, large–small, high–low, broad–narrow.
Position: It is characterised through the position in space: lying, sitting, kneeling, standing, squatting.
Levels: These are determined by the position of the centre of gravity:
e.g.   Low: knees bent, low-placed centre of gravity.
        Medium: feet flat on the floor, centre of gravity as for walking.
        High: standing on the balls of the feet, legs stretched, high-placed centre of gravity.
Direction of gaze: The focus can be:
constant in the direction of the movement;
constant in any direction other than that of the movement;
changing between up and down, right and left, etc.
Movement paths: There are fundamentally only two kinds of paths possible, straight or curved.

Basic forms of straight movement paths

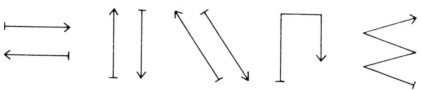

Variations on straight movement paths (each side can consist of one or more steps)

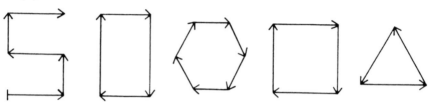

Basic forms of curved paths
circle--snake--free curves

Variations on curved paths
spiral--figure of eight--various shapes

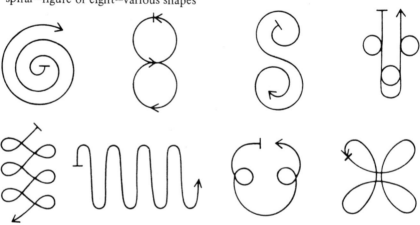

All these movement paths can be executed by individuals, pairs, chains etc. Curved and straight paths can also be combined.

Formations and group arrangements

Straight line basic forms

Chain: standing one behind the other   Row: standing beside one another

Basic straight line forms varied through different formations

Chains in open form

   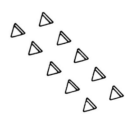

Rows in open form

69

Chains or rows in closed form

Basic curved shapes

circle--semicircle or arc

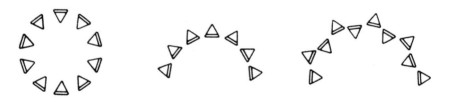

Variations on basic curved shapes

Double circle--double semicircle--various arrangements of circles and semicircles

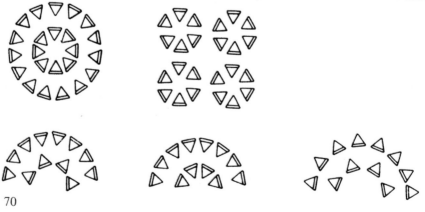

Pair formations

next to one another, front facing same direction or in opposite directions

opposite or diagonally opposite

one behind the other or back to back

Formations in threes

next to one another as a row   behind one another as a chain

in a triangle

Group formations

front facing forwards   facing the centre   facing outwards

71

Various ways of holding: Individual formations can be given variety through various holds. The most useful are given here.

Holding with one hand

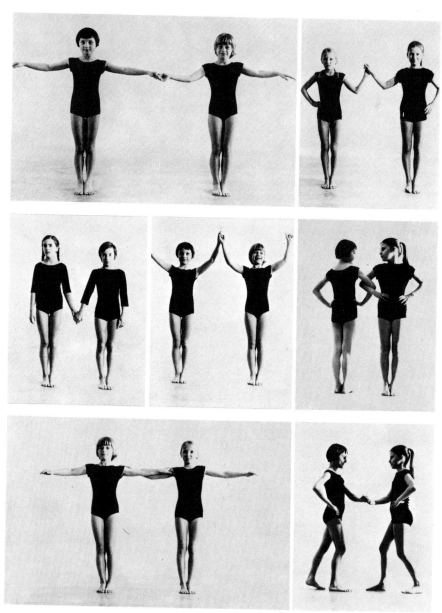

Holding with both hands

Time

Every movement can be looked at from different aspects of time.

Tempo:
slow, moderately fast, fast
accelerando (continuously increasing speed)
ritardando (continuously decreasing speed)
sudden change (doubling or halving) of tempo
rubato (arbitrary variations of tempo)

Even or uneven movement flow: A movement can be made over an even pulse
(that does not have to be audible) so that the same amount of travelling
distance takes the same amount of time. The movement flow can also be uneven
so that more time is taken for one movement and less for another.

Even walking   Uneven walking

Even double bounce   Uneven double bounce (skipping)

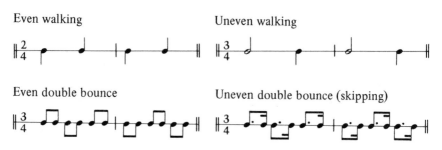

Uneven units, when repeated, can form an even sequence.

Making rhythmic structures: Movement motifs that are metric in character can
result from the combination of movements of varying lengths. A particular step
can, according to the purpose of the movement, take on different rhythmic
phrasings.

Change step   Change step with a different rhythmic structure

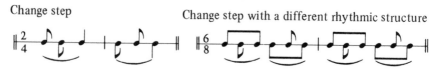

Different time units and phrases including changes of time unit: The character of
a movement is variable according to the kind of time unit in which it is

performed. An erect walk in four-four time is clearly different, for instance, from a swinging one in six-eight time. Movement combinations that are rich in contrast and that are particularly attractive result from phrases that include changes of time unit.

Swinging walk with stamped close

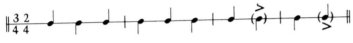

Dynamics

The dynamics of a movement are dependent on *use of weight, inner intensity* and *muscular tension*. The resulting movement quality can be described as: relaxed, delicate, soft, light, fleeting; or as strong, tense, powerful, heavy, energetic. *Sudden changes of tension, continuous changes of tension* (e.g. crescendo or decrescendo) and *regular* or *irregular placing of accents* are further aspects of the dynamics of movement.

The reciprocal influences of the factors of space, time and dynamics and their effect on movement can be shown in one example.

Walking, through a change of tempo (accelerando) becomes running; through increased dynamic contribution an intensive pressing-up from the floor and simultaneous emphasis on a more elevated movement follows; the steps become shorter in length and the locomotion occurs in an upwards direction and is springy in character. Through a change of direction from forwards to sideways step-close or cross-over steps will arise. The development can be continued at will. The occasional changing of only one factor results in a clearly recognisable change in the movement itself.

Summary of various types of movement (characteristics, faults and corrections)

The characterisation of movement is rendered more difficult by the varied and sometimes contradictory versions given in different countries and schools. The only complete analysis of movement relevant to dance, sport and work is that evolved by Rudolf von Laban. With the help of his 'Kinetography' (movement notation) these movements can be notated. The Laban movement notation demands intensive study; it goes far beyond anything with which a nursery or primary school teacher is likely to be confronted. With regard to the practical problems that arise in teaching, a simplified presentation of the characteristics of movement, of the possibilities for variation in the ways of moving, and of the principal faults and their corrections will be attempted in the following account.

The setting of tasks that result from the basic forms, both individually and in combination, is particularly important for practical purposes. They must cover the movement aspects of space, time, dynamics and group relationships. Through such tasks children become aware, without their knowing it, of possible variations on an initial movement impulse and thereby realise the expressive qualities arising from these aspects. Solutions to such tasks can sometimes produce examples that the teacher might normally reject as 'wrong' or 'wasteful of energy' and that may even be classified as main faults. The children should nevertheless be free to experiment as much as possible in order to train their sense of movement and their imagination. In comparing the solutions it will soon become clear to them which of these may seem funny but very tiring or even painful after a while, and which are the most appropriate, practical or the most attractive.

Examples using walking will show the type of task under consideration:

—*Tasks in awareness of space:* How can one travel along the diagonal and arrive in the far corner of the room with the minimum of steps, and without jumping or running? And with many short steps? Each child should travel along a certain path (curved or straight). What does it look like if, while walking, one makes oneself very tall or very small? What happens then to the legs or the trunk? Which part of the foot touches the ground first when we walk? And when we walk backwards? How can one perform a skilful change from walking forwards to walking backwards? When does a change of direction come about (e.g. through turning sideways or turning round)? How can one walk sideways? Who can see, while walking, the whole room, the ceiling and the other children without coming off course (changing focus of eyes)? Who can play with a ball or on a tambour while walking?

—*Tasks in awareness of time:* Who walks very slowly and who very fast What does the one or the other look like? Who can walk in the way that a drum or some other instrument sounds (in time, or following the rhythmic pattern or the dynamics)? How does one walk evenly, and how unevenly (limping, change-step)? Who can make a rhythmic pattern in their walking and at the same time clap to it? How fast can one walk without it becoming running? Who can start together with the accompaniment and stop when it stops? Who can change their direction when the melody repeats itself?

—*Tasks in dynamics:* Who can walk so quietly that one hears nothing? What is it like when one makes very firm, energetic steps? When does one need more energy--when one pulls or pushes someone, or when one leads him almost without touching him at all? How can one make regular or irregular accents when walking?

—*Tasks in group relationships:* The children walk freely around the room without bumping into one another; while walking they should find a partner or form a small group; this breaks up and a new one is formed; one partner leads or is led (with or without holding one another). How can one change the leader of a chain without coming to a standstill? In how many different ways can a group of three hold on to one another?

—*Tasks in impersonation:* Each child can imagine someone and show how he would move along: prowling like a Red Indian; the heavy tread of the collier carrying coal; walking with a stick; walking cautiously as if on ice; walking carefully, carrying something precious on the head; the leisurely walk of some-one going for a stroll. The results are compared and individual impersonations can be interpreted in different ways.

The general examples, related only to the action of walking and not specifically confined to any particular age group, show how it is possible to devise tasks out of certain movement characteristics. Naturally the same principles are applicable to all other forms of movement. The formulation and content of the task should relate to the age and understanding of the children.

Locomotor movements

To these belong walking, running, skipping, trotting, jumping (but also creeping, crawling, rolling, travelling on all fours, cartwheeling etc.). We shall limit ourselves here to the principal forms that are met most frequently in children's elemental dance.

Walking

General characteristics

A trained and observant teacher can discover much about the psychological attitude of her pupils through observing them walking, a form of locomotion natural to all physically normal people.

Walking consists of carrying the weight over from one leg to the other, the leg that is moving forward passing in close proximity to the supporting leg (knee and hip joints slightly bent). The placing of the foot is dependent upon the direction of the step--in the natural forward walk the foot rolls from the heel to the ball and then to the pushing-off pressure of the toes; in the stylised forward walk and also in walking backwards the foot rolls in the opposite way, from the ball to the heel. The size of the step depends on the pushing-off pressure of the active leg and the extent of the forward reach. The body is upright, the eyes directed towards one's destination and the arms swing loosely in contrary motion.

Variations: Walking on the heels, on the toes and on the outside edge of the foot in alternation; with knees straight, extremely bent or drawn up high; with noiseless, sliding steps or with stamps; leading with the working leg in different ways; with straight or bent trunk; with legs turned inwards or outwards; with or without the inclusion of arm movements.

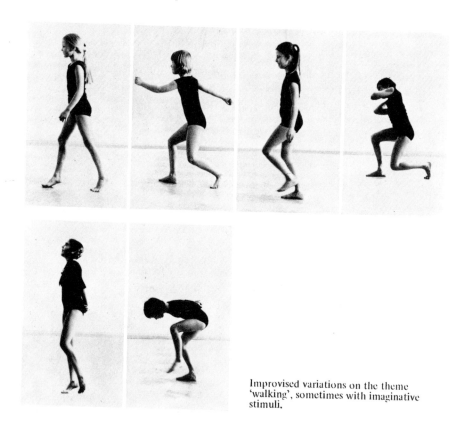

Improvised variations on the theme 'walking', sometimes with imaginative stimuli.

Summary
Space: Directions are forwards, backwards, to the right, to the left (sideways movement achieved with cross-over step or side and close) and turning (with one or more steps); straight or curved movement paths in free or geometric figures; steps spaced narrowly or widely; centre of gravity normal, low and high; focus of eyes facing direction of movement or free.
Time: From slow to fast speed (children have a faster normal speed than adults); accelerando and ritardando or sudden changes of tempo; regular or irregular; different rhythms, in time units with an even and with an odd number of beats, also without fixed metre, with and without accompaniment.
Dynamics: From light to energetic; continuous or sudden changes of intensity; regular or irregular accents.
Group relationships: Alone (orientation in the room, adaptation to other children in the room, avoidance of obstacles); in pairs in various relationships and different ways of holding one another, similarly in threes and in smaller or larger groups, in chains, rows, circles.

Main faults and corrections

Only the most common faults can be described here; those that are more serious are referred for remedial exercises or to a doctor.

—Tense walking with knees pressed back and stiff arms: the cause of this is not necessarily physical, the child may be particularly anxious and movement shy. This faulty posture is often caused by the exaggerated, desperate striving to do especially well. Casual, sauntering walking with plenty of rise and fall combined with the help of imaginative stimuli may serve as a counterbalance. Praise and encouragement will help to ease the tension.

—Turning the foot too much inwards or outwards: make them conscious of the fault through trying to walk like a 'duck' or like a 'clown'. Walk at first along a real, and then along an imaginary line on the floor.

—Fallen arches (flat feet) or too strong a tendency to walk on the outside of the foot (turning the ankles over): these faults can only be eliminated through careful and continuous exercises. In serious cases the advice of an orthopaedic specialist should be sought.

—Straddling, walking with the feet far apart so that they are not placed one in front of the other, but rather diagonally: walking along a long bench or plank, along a rope or along a chalk line on the floor may make the child aware of this fault and help to remove it.

—Walking heavily on the heels or dragging the feet and making a shuffling noise: show this slipshod fault in exaggeration so that it is recognised. Then give exercises that stress lifting the foot, think of imaginative stimuli that induce quiet walking and make the child aware of the correct rolling action of the foot.

—Poor posture characterised by the top of the body drooping forwards: this can be a sign of extreme tiredness, but it is mostly a persistent weakness of posture. In this case the appropriate exercises must be intensified. Games involving the carrying of books, bean bags, drums on the head, or other imaginative stimuli can draw attention to the posture.

The more we improve the development of the body and the teaching of good posture, the less frequently such faults arise. In any case correction should be started as soon as possible. This should take the form of a suitable game and the teacher's attitude should be friendly. The ill-famed phrase 'hold yourself properly' has little effect.

Running

General characteristics

Running comes about through a rapid transfer of the weight of the body from one leg to the other, while for a moment, between taking off from one leg and landing on the other, the body remains in the air without support. In landing the foot rolls from the ball over the whole foot, the heel lightly touching the floor (rolling from heel to toe produces a clumsy run with short steps). By reaching forward with the working leg—dependent on mobility of the hip joint—a run with long steps is achieved. The trunk leans slightly forwards, the eyes focus in the direction of travel, the arms, slightly bent at the elbows, swing backwards and forwards beside the body.

Besides this basic form there are some especially characteristic ways of running:

Bouncing run: Here the emphasis is generally upwards (only in exceptional cases downwards), the steps are mostly short, the bouncing movement from one leg to the other being very similar; in movement quality it can be compared with staccato.

Swinging run: Mostly in three-four, six-eight or nine-eight time. Through the grouping of beats in uneven numbers the accent comes on alternate feet. This produces the swinging character that can be emphasised through a slight bending of the trunk over the accented step. The length of step is either

Running with a forwards impulse, phase of pushing-off and follow-through.

80

uniform or the first and accented step is long and the others are shorter. The hands are on the hips or the arms are stretched out to the sides. Hanging or swinging arms hamper the movement. The swinging run is specially suited to girls who have an already well-developed feeling for movement. In the primary school, therefore, it is mostly introduced only to the older girls. The movement quality is comparable to legato.

Leaping: This is a particularly powerful run. The pressure from the supporting leg is very intensive, so that the body remains a little longer in the air and the working leg has time to reach out and stretch forward. The landing should be supple and silent. The arms swing in opposition. Leaping is particularly suitable for boys.

Variations: The knee of the working leg can be bent and drawn up high or the heel can be lifted behind so that it almost touches the buttocks. The working leg can also be flung sideways. The upper part of the body can be held upright or can be deliberately swayed forwards and backwards. Also, according to the character of the movement the arms can be held stretched sideways, placed on the hips or swung freely in opposition.

Summary

Space: Directions are forwards (also with turns), backwards, sideways (only with cross-over step alternately in front and behind); change of direction; pathways that are straight or in narrow or broad curves that bend inwards, seldom outwards; length of step from short (tripping along) to long (leaping); centre of gravity normal, low and high; focus of eyes normally in the direction of travel, for special reasons towards other directions or free to wander.

Time: The normal running tempo is admittedly faster than a walking tempo but certainly not twice as fast, as is often asserted; speed should range from fairly slow (big steps) to very fast tripping along; gradual or sudden changes of tempo, rubato; the use of rhythmic patterns interrupts the flow of the movement; in different time units; with or without accompaniment.

Dynamics: From light and bouncing to powerful and leaping; emphasis of the movement upwards or forwards in the direction of travel; steps accented regularly or irregularly.

Group relationships: Singly, in pairs, in threes, in smaller or larger groups, with or without touching or holding (the closer the hold the more difficult it is to follow or to lead); in chains and rows with change of leader.

Main faults and corrections

—Loud and clumsy running on the whole foot without the rolling action: supple landing and elasticity in all joints is not yet sufficiently developed. Exercises to increase flexibility and strength of foot are needed. It is often, however, a case of lack of attention on the part of a child and the fault can be corrected simply by pointing it out.

—Audible shuffling of the feet: the lifting of the working leg must be made stronger; the child can be made aware of it by drawing up the knee extremely high.

—Increasing the speed when running backwards: the body leans too far backwards and the legs seem to slip away from beneath the centre of gravity; in order to prevent falling the steps become increasingly faster. When the legs step out backwards with big steps and the foot, landing first on the toes, rolls over the ball onto the heel, the weight of the body must be shifted slightly forwards for balance.

—Flaccid running with poor posture and eyes looking at the ground: this posture mostly shows movement inhibition and an inner lack of energy that cannot be corrected by posture exercises alone. Often it is merely a question of temporary tiredness that can be overcome by changing the theme (e.g. exercises with a partner) the change acting as a new incentive.

—Running with the pelvis pushed forwards: the upper part of the body leans too far backwards and consequently the pelvis is pushed forwards as a counterbalance. To draw attention to the forwards and backwards slope of the upper part of the body, experiment with shifting its weight in different degrees until the right angle of slope has been found.

Bouncing

General characteristics

By bouncing is meant, primarily, a quick and light bending and straightening of any joint; the movement can occur with or without weight-bearing. It can either be a movement that is fading out until it comes to rest, or continuous movement that is maintained by constant muscular drive. Bouncing exercises for ankle, knee and hip joints are an essential preparation for all running, skipping and jumping exercises. They contribute to elasticity and strength. Bouncing as a means of locomotion develops out of exercises on the spot, the preparatory moving up and down of the heels with feet together. Ankle, knee and hip joints are under stress during the bending; when stretching either legs or trunk, the heels are lifted from the floor. The pushing away from the floor can become increasingly stronger until finally the toes leave the floor. When landing, a gentle rolling movement of the foot is required.

One distinguishes between:

—Bouncing (moving heels up and down) with feet together (in the squatting position or standing upright)
—Single bounce: from one foot to the other
—Double bounce: twice on one foot, then twice on the other
—Triple or multiple bounce: on each foot and then a transfer of weight to the other (the change need not be regular).

All the above forms of bouncing can be practised either on the spot or in locomotion.

Variations: Varied positions for the working leg; it can be bent or straight in knee or ankle and can be held forwards, backwards, sideways or across the other leg; the toes or heel of the working leg can touch the floor lightly or powerfully. Regular or irregular shifting from one leg to the other is possible. For the position of the trunk and arms the same possibilities exist as in walking and running.

Bouncing in the squatting position   Bouncing from one leg to the other

Summary

Space: Directions are forwards, backwards, sideways (with cross-over or side and close), turning; in locomotion and on the spot; movement paths are straight (good for zigzag) or in small curves; length of step mainly short, seldom long; centre of gravity mostly medium and high, seldom low; focus of eyes mostly in the direction of travel, seldom changing.

Time: From relatively slow tempo (requires much energy) to fairly rapid (for beginners a medium speed is the most suitable); various rhythmic patterns; in all known time-signatures and in phrases containing changes of time-signature (through the combination of single and multiple bouncing); bouncing twice and evenly on each foot at regular intervals is called even double bouncing, bouncing twice and unevenly on each foot (in a dotted rhythm) is called uneven double bouncing, or skipping (see music examples on p. 74).

Dynamics: Light, sprightly, from elastic to energetic and with emphasis upwards or in direction of travel; the change from light and unstressed to strong and well-accented bouncing can also be practised in a constant tempo.

Group relationships: Alone, in twos, threes or in small or large groups (chains, rows), in various formations with uniform or different movement directions; close holding positions (by the waist or on the shoulders) require very good adaptation in the size of the steps and the amount of upward drive.

Main faults and corrections

—Excessive exertion in the push-up from the floor causing a tense posture: the attempt at bouncing particularly high, with insufficient body control, easily results in a loss of balance in the inexperienced child. Concentrating on low and regular bouncing is more effective at this stage.

—Noisy landing on the whole foot without any give, turning the ankles over:

83

the strength and elasticity needed for bouncing are not yet sufficiently developed. Bouncing with a drive that is upwards or in the direction of travel can only be attempted when the ankle joint has been sufficiently strengthened through repeated preparatory exercises.

—When changing between forwards and backwards bouncing the backward movement uses less space than the corresponding forward movement: the working leg needs to be thrust far enough backwards from the thigh. This movement is prepared at a slower speed in walking, then increased to bouncing.

—Upper body leaning forwards and with rounded shoulders: often caused by weak back muscles and an insufficient ability to straighten the trunk. Intensified posture training is necessary. This can be helped by imagining one is carrying something in the hands or on the head. The focus of the eyes should be in the direction of travel or, when working with a partner, towards him.

—Remaining floor-bound: lack of tension in the pelvis and too little elasticity in the leg that is pushing-up from the floor may be the cause. Sometimes the teacher's incorrect accompaniment is the cause. It is the pushing-off action and not the landing that is accented.

Skipping

General characteristics

Skipping is used extensively in the teaching of beginners; for this reason it is described here in detail as a basic form of movement. Terminologically it is a (smaller or larger) hop from one foot onto the same foot. As with double bouncing the same foot touches the floor twice in succession before a transfer of weight takes place. The body is shot into the air by the action of the supporting leg (the working leg can be drawn up at the knee, slightly bent, the foot is more or less stretched). The landing occurs on the leg from which the hop was made and the working leg steps out and becomes in its turn the supporting leg. The trunk is upright, the eyes focus in the direction of travel, the arms swing in opposition.

Three phases
of skipping

84

One distinguishes between the following ways of skipping:

Simple skip or "children's skip": This is the simplest form of skipping that is used by all children. The bent free leg is drawn up and the foot is (not excessively) stretched. This form of movement is familiar to all young school children, including even those of nursery school age.

Swinging skip: Mostly in three-four, six-eight or similar time. The working leg is not drawn up high, but with a slightly bent knee is swung forwards or backwards or is crossed over the supporting leg either in front or behind.

Long or upward skip: According to the movement impulse the skip can be very flat and therefore with long steps, or especially high and then with shorter steps. A combination of both upward and forward impelled skipping is possible with children whose jumping capacity has been well-developed.

Variations: The movement impulse (particularly using a lower step—with bent knees—or a longer step) as well as the way the working leg is held (stretched, bent, crossed over, out to the side) can be changed, as can also the normal posture of the upper body and arms.

Summary

Space: On the spot (upward skip); directions are forwards, backwards (somewhat more difficult), sideways (as a skipped cross-over or step and close), turning and with change of direction; using curved and straight movement paths; with small or large steps; with centre of gravity at a medium level (long skip) or high; focus in the direction of travel or eyes wandering freely.

Skipping turning on the spot

Time: In relatively slow or fast tempo; in dotted or triplet rhythm; in different kinds of time units, with or without accompaniment.

Skipping

Dynamics: From light to energetic; simple combinations of speed and dynamics are as follows: light and fast or strong and slow. With those who are more advanced the combinations light and slow, strong and fast can also be practised.

Group relationships: Singly, in pairs, in threes or more, beside, behind or opposite one another; holding on to one another in different ways, also in chains, rows or in a circle (a close hold makes difficulties for beginners).

Main faults and corrections

In practically every group we find one or more children who have initial difficulties with skipping. In this case a good demonstration of the movement can be very helpful. The teacher or the more skilled children skip with the "stragglers"; in general they are suddenly able to do it. Oppressive or forcible practising is not recommended. Faults in skipping are essentially very similar to those of bouncing, as far as posture, take-off and landing are concerned.

—Imprecise skipping: the required energy impulse is not correctly assessed. If it is too big the landing comes late, if it is too small the children skip faster than the accompaniment and cannot fill out the time. It is therefore best to skip without accompaniment at first; later the teacher takes the tempo from individual children. Only after this stage is a rhythmic accompaniment given and the children asked to keep time to it.

Jumping

General characteristics

Jumping is developed from running, bouncing and skipping. Through the intensity of the take-off the body finds itself unsupported in the air for a moment, it "flies". Overcoming the force of gravity, even if only for a moment, makes jumping a special experience.

A well-developed resilience, a powerful thrust in take-off, ability to make a supple landing and a sure posture are preconditions for jumping. Only when these conditions have been brought about can one begin to practise jumping, otherwise severe foot injury can be caused.

We can distinguish five forms of jumping:*

—from one foot onto the other (leap)

—from one foot onto both feet (e.g. assemblé)

—from one foot onto the same foot (e.g. turning hop, skip, heel-click jump)

—from both feet onto both feet (e.g. sitting jump, sauté)

—from both feet onto one foot (e.g. sissonne)

Only the most common jumps, that can be started with children, are given below. As a rule both the right and the left foot should have practice as the "take-off foot".

---

*Apart from the leap and the hop there are no convenient English labels for the basic jumps. Their variations have been given specific names for the sake of clarity. Where appropriate some ballet terms have also been used. Descriptions of each jump can be found in the text below.

Run and leap: This leap occurs after a few running steps and an especially strong thrust from the supporting leg; the body is shot into the air, the working leg stretching forward as far as possible. At the climax of the jump one leg is stretched forwards, the other backwards, the trunk is inclined slightly in the direction of travel, i.e. forwards, the arms swing in opposition or are held at the sides. Leaps are best practised by taking a preparatory run and then jumping over small, harmless obstacles (e.g. articles of clothing). Jumps without the preparatory running steps in between are very strenuous and should only be introduced when a good facility for jumping has been developed.

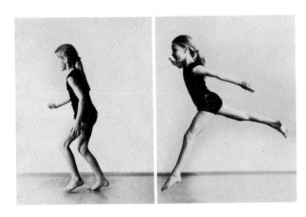

Preparatory run and leap

In combining leaps with running steps care should be taken that both feet have practice at "taking off". With an even number of intermediate steps the take-off foot alternates between right and left; with an uneven number it remains the same. In the latter case therefore the sequence must be repeated, first with the right foot and then the next time with the left.

Leaping from the same foot

Leaping from alternate feet

Scissor-jump: This can be executed with straight or with bent legs (gallop jump). After the take-off the working leg is thrown high in the direction of travel, the second leg follows into the same position so that both legs remain thus in the air for a moment. On landing the weight is taken by the leg that was formerly the working leg.

Scissor-jump taking off from the same foot

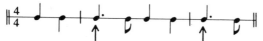

Scissor-jump taking off from alternate feet

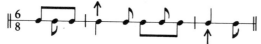

Scissor-jump (with straight legs) and gallop jump (with bent legs) are best suited to forwards movement or to turns. The one with straight legs produces a wider turning jump, that with bent legs a narrower one. Both are relatively difficult to do backwards.

Jump from one foot to two feet: For children this is one of the simplest jumps. From standing, walking, running or bouncing the supporting leg pushes the body upwards, the working leg is thrown in the direction of travel followed by a landing on both feet, the feet rolling from ball to heel without sound and with a slight give in all leg joints. This jump can be executed in all directions (forwards, backwards, sideways and turning). It is generally used as the final jump of a phrase. Should it be used continuously, however, (with or without preparatory steps) either foot can initiate the take-off following each landing. These jumps (according to the children's capacity) can be made in quarter, half or whole turns.

Jumping from one to two feet taking off from the same foot

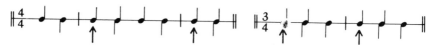

Jumping form one to two feet taking off from alternate feet

Heel-click jump: This jump from one foot onto the same foot is more difficult. Before landing, with the legs straight (also, but less often, with bent legs) the heels click together, usually to the side, but also forwards or backwards. The working leg strikes down from above, the other up from below. In contrast to the jump from one to two feet the landing is made only on the take-off foot. Preparatory exercise: hop on the right leg, travelling towards the direction of the working leg which is lifted slightly to the side. Then begin trying to touch the two heels lightly together before landing.

Preparatory exercise for heel-click jump

Heel-click jump with intermediate steps

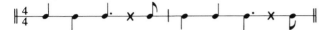

Turning jump: Nearly all jumps can turn (see scissor-jump, jump from one to two feet, hop). The term "turning jump" usually means a jump that develops from a step that causes the body to turn (e.g. "grand jeté en tournant" of ballet). The preparation can be a forwards or a sideways movement and can be achieved in two ways:

a) While walking or running (this works best in three-four time with a clear stress on the first beat of the bar) a half turn is made between the first and second step (the second step therefore being taken backwards) and the turn is completed between the second and third step (the third step being taken forwards in the original direction). The turn is practised to the right and the left. As soon as the turn is mastered in this way it can be done with a jump. Through a strong take-off from the first foot a turning jump is made between the first and second step, thus changing the rhythm and allowing more time for the turn.

Preparation for a turning jump forwards

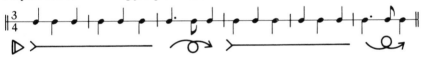

b) The turn is prepared by a sideways movement (cross-over or step and close) at first without, then with a jump.

Preparation for a turning jump sideways

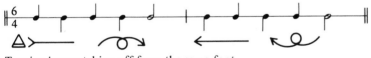

Turning jumps taking off from the same foot

Turning jumps taking off from alternate feet

Turning jumps in pairs

Turning hop: Take-off and landing use the same foot. The turning develops from a hop with the working leg held straight. This working leg is swung forwards and held there while the supporting leg and the trunk twist round through 180 degrees. The working leg is now stretched out behind the body. To prepare the turn stand in pairs. The right leg is lifted forwards with straight knee and held by the partner. Turn on the left leg to the opposite direction until the held leg is behind the body; return on the same path to face forwards once more. Then try to turn with a slight jump, without the help of a partner and while travelling. After the jump the working leg always becomes the new supporting leg.

Turning hop taking off from the same foot

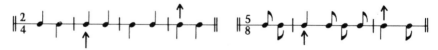

Turning hop taking off from alternate feet

Sauté: This jump, from two feet to two feet, demands some strength. Children, especially boys, perform it with enthusiasm. It is usually done on the spot but can also come at the end of a run.

Sitting jump: After the take-off from both feet the knees are brought up as near to the chest as possible and the arms can clasp the knees at the same time. The landing must nevertheless be quiet and supple.

Sideways splits jump: After taking off from both feet the legs are opened sideways as far as possible.

Splits jump: After taking off from both feet the legs are opened forwards and backwards as far as possible.

On account of their difficulty and the strength they require splits jumps should only be practised with advanced pupils. Every ambition to jump as high as possible and to split the legs as wide as possible is often achieved at the expense of posture and controlled landing.

Jump from two feet onto one: After the take-off from both feet the landing occurs on only one. If the direction of the jump is forwards the free leg is stretched out backwards, and vice versa. The jump can also be made sideways. The free leg always points in the opposite direction to that of the jump.

Variations: When training the necessary strength for jumping and when working at specific jumps the specialised jumps should not be over-emphasised. Children should at first experience jumping in as many different ways as possible, gradually developing skill through jumping off low-level apparatus such as forms or stools (the stool being held by another child so that it cannot slip); jumping over small obstacles (no rolling objects like balls or canes or accidents may result); jumping up high from a run and touching, with hands or head, objects held by the teacher or a partner (a cloth, taut rope, tambour); jumping with preparatory run or from standing.

Improvised variations on the theme "jumping"

Summary

Space: Forwards direction (leap, scissor-jump, jumps from one to two feet, heel-click jump); backwards (jumps from one to two feet, turning hop, less often heel-click jump and scissor-jump); sideways (jumps from one to two feet, heel-click jump); turning (scissor-jump, jumps from one to two feet and turning jump, with the turning hop a half turn is always produced).

All jumps which take up a lot of space are best performed on a straight pathway, but other kinds of movement paths can also be used through incorporating phrases of intermediate steps. Most jumps have an emphasis on either height or length. Landings can follow-through down to a squatting position. The eyes should focus in the direction of travel; looking down should be discouraged. *Time:* The preparatory run occurs mostly on the up-beat, the take-off coming on the down beat (with the strongest emphasis). In order to make the landing as light as possible, heavy stress should be avoided on that beat in the accompaniment. For both high and long jumps the tempo must be correspondingly slow, for short and low jumps it can be somewhat faster. A rhythmic pattern will arise from the way in which the jumps are interspersed with travelling steps. This can also change the number of beats in a bar and phrases that include changes of time signature can be used. A great variety of combinations of steps and jumps should also be practised in free rhythm and without accompaniment. *Dynamics:* Of all activities jumping requires the most energy. This does not start in the take off, but begins rather in the preparatory run, increasing up to the jump and only releasing the tension a little just after the landing. Care must be taken to ensure that the children do not get exhausted while jumping. Jumps must be performed with apparent ease in spite of the energy that they require. *Group relationships:* Generally speaking, when working on jumping in a group, the varying amounts of vigour used tend to hinder some less secure children. Nevertheless, while working at the heel-click and turning jumps children can always help each other by offering a forearm as a support to a jumping child. Admittedly most other jumps can be performed lined up side by side or behind one another, but any kind of hold should be avoided until the jumps themselves have become reliable and steady. This can most easily be achieved with the jump from one to two feet and the scissor-jump.

Main faults and corrections

Most mistakes in jumping come from insufficient preparation. The ability to jump will come from good resilience. Consequently it is in this sphere that preparation is needed.

--Hard, jerky landing: lacking in resistance during the rolling action of the foot, too little flexibility in knee and hip joint.

--Difficulties with balance; upper part of body leans forwards, backwards or sideways: an excessively ambitious effort thrusts the whole body in the direction of the jump. This results in a loss of balance. Small, light jumps with good posture are better and more effective than large ones that are spoilt by "wobbling".

--Co-ordination difficulties in combining jumps with intermediate steps: the movement sequence is often too long or too complicated. Individual elements should be practised and then put together, first into small combinations and only later into longer ones.

General characteristics

Turning is not really an independent form of movement, but a particular spatial extension of walking, running and jumping, in which the body turns round its own longitudinal axis. It can be combined with the different forms of locomotion (e.g. rolling on the ground) or can be done on the spot (standing, sitting, kneeling), in a small circle or on straight or curved paths about the room.

Turning on the spot

Every child very soon discovers simple spinning on the spot. With arms spread wide he turns round his own axis until he feels giddy, staggers and falls down. In spite of the fall he practises this movement again and again as if intoxicated by the experience. Many ritual-ecstatic dances are whirling dances (e.g. the whirling dances of the Dervishes)

Turning while sitting
Turning on the spot, low and high level

Whirling: This is a continuous turning in one direction with many small steps using the sole or just the ball of the foot. Whirling can turn in one direction only or it can change direction after a sudden or gradual stop. We distinguish two ways of doing this:

Turning with step and close: One turns with many tiny repetitions of step and close so that the heels remain as near as possible on one spot and the leading foot is turned slightly outwards as it steps. For a whole turn as many steps as desired may be used, but one can also try exact eighth, quarter or half-turns.

Turning with cross-over steps: A preliminary exercise for this is the transfer of weight in the cross-over step. Stand with the weight on the right foot, the left foot crossed behind, on the ball of the foot without weight. The weight is now transferred alternately between the back and front foot. Eventually the front foot steps out a little in the direction of the turn (i.e. the right foot to the right or the left to the left). This turn, which revolves round the back foot as centre, can be performed with an arbitrary, or with an absolutely precise number of steps.

Turning on one foot: This can be done either with repeated hopping on one foot (i.e. left leg supporting, left shoulder leading in backward turn), or with a swing on the sole of the foot (i.e. left leg steps out to the side and left shoulder follows through with a backward swing). Outward turns are more suitable for children than inward turns. In both ways given above the free leg can be straight or bent at the knee as in the simple skip.

All turns on the spot are best practised with many small steps or bounces, so that each time only an eighth of a turn is accomplished. Later, quarter and half turns can be attempted, and with the cross-over step and hopping a whole turn can be attempted. These turns can occur at one level (low, middle or high), but they can also be "spiralled" from low to high or from high to low. The arms give the impetus for these turns.

Turns while travelling

Quarter, half or whole turns can be incorporated into walking, running and skipping. One can turn equally well towards the supporting leg as towards the free leg. An *outward turn* occurs when one turns on the right leg (supporting leg) to the right, or on the left leg to the left.

An *inward turn* occurs when one turns on the right leg (supporting leg) to the left and on the left leg to the right.

Quarter turns: The moment at which the turn is made is decisive for whether a movement path is to be travelled with outward or inward turns. Two examples illustrate this:

Quarter turn in zig-zag: The outward turn takes place on the third step, that is at the end of each straight line.

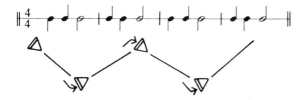

Quarter turns in a square: Alternate outward and inward turns, the first step starts each time in the new direction.

Half turns: While travelling forwards a half turn is made (outwards or inwards). With continued travelling the direction can either be maintained—in which case the next step is taken backwards (example a)—or the direction changes but the dancer continues to travel forwards after the half turn, thus retracing her path (example b).

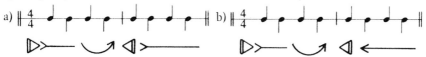

Whole turns: These are practised preferably as outward turns and they can be spread over one or more steps (see turning jump, p. 89). The turn on one foot can be made bouncing or hopping, first on the sole and later on the ball of the foot. *Turning while travelling sideways:* This takes place continuously in one direction (here the turn can be inward or outward, or alternately inward and outward) or with change of direction from one side to the other. Children find outward turns with a change of direction or continuous outward turns in the same direction easiest. Two examples illustrate this:
a) Outward turn with change of direction: Step right foot to the side, take half a turn on the right foot, left foot closes to it taking the weight. The return path is just the same, right steps out, half turn, left closes and takes weight.

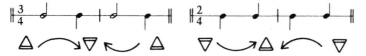

b) Continuous outward turns: Step right foot to the side, half turn, close left to it without taking weight. For the next, step left foot to the side, half turn, right foot closes to it without weight.

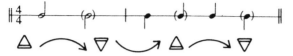

Combinations of side steps, half turns with change of direction and continuous half turns should be worked out.

Whole turns can also be made outwards or inwards, outwards being easier. The turn is made on the first step, with a well turned-out working leg; at the end of the turn the second foot closes to the first and takes the weight. These turns are relatively difficult and are best combined with a sequence of closing-up steps.

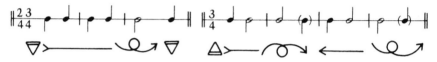

Waltz turn: This turn is made in two halves, each half taking three steps. The first step is taken forwards, the second and third complete the half turn; the fourth step is backwards, the fifth and sixth complete the turn. Steps one and four are stressed and somewhat larger.

In this example the first half turn occurs forwards over the right foot, the second backwards over the left foot.

Movement variations: Swinging or quiet turns with various ways of bringing about the change of direction (letting it fade, stopping abruptly with a stamp or a hop); holding the free leg in different ways when turning on one leg; arms in a fixed position, arms lifted by centrifugal force or actively contributing to the swing, also arms opening and closing with the turn; trunk upright or leaning forwards.

Summary
Space: On the spot and travelling (in a straight line, ina circle, in narrow or wide curves); forwards, backwards or sideways, inwards or outwards; at low, middle or high levels and as spiral turns moving through all three levels; focus in the direction of the turn, eyes fixed for as long as possible on one point and then the quick turn of the head; looking up, down or straight ahead can be

attempted, but this makes the turn much more difficult.

Time: Tempo remaining constant, slow or fast; accelerando or ritardando; in metric or free rhythm; with or without accompaniment; in different rhythmic structures (even and uneven steps) and in different time units; turning in three-four or six-eight time has more swing than in two-four or four-four.

Dynamics: The swing of a turn depends upon the impetus used in its preparation; it can have an even dynamic level or it can be maintained and driven on by repeated fresh impulses. The direction can be changed after the impulse has died away. The type of movement and the tempo at which it is performed are dependent upon the input of energy. A quick turn in the air needs more energy than a quiet one using even walking steps. Variety and extremes in dynamic quality should be explored.

Group formations: In pairs holding each other with both hands (as in "twizzling"); with one hand (both using the same hand, e.g. the right), when changing directions the hands must also be changed; with one hand (inside hand) when beside one another, here the hands are released when turning; in threes holding with one hand, e.g. the right. (Turns under the arms are possible when holding loosely. The hold is dependent on the kind of turn and hands may have to be released.)

Main faults and corrections

—Loss of orientation: Only a few people can turn without any feeling of giddiness, but it can be reduced when the eyes are focussed for as long as possible on a point in the direction of the turn. After turning (in order to recover) one should not shut the eyes but make a quick turn in the opposite direction and then stand still, fixing the gaze on some point.

—Overspinning: The swing of the turn is greater than needed. Children often spin with too much energy because they are afraid they will not turn far enough.

—Not turning far enough: There is not enough impetus for the turn. To give confidence one can occasionally help with a small push. Turning "with all their might" should only seldom be tried, for children lose their balance and cannot control the ending. Generally speaking whole turns should only be worked at when half turns are fully under control.

—Insecure finish to the turn: Balance and energy of the swing are not adjusted. Turns can be finished in many different ways. It is often wise to suspend the flow just before the end, to "brake" with the heels against the floor and to concentrate the gaze on one point.

Body swaying with transfer of weight

This type of movement is mainly a development from moving on the spot and it can be extended to become locomotion. Swaying with transfer of weight will therefore be found under the heading "Movement on the spot".

Movement on the spot

Included here are all the movements of the head, neck, trunk, arms and legs in bending, straightening, spreading sideways, closing in, turning inwards, outwards and sideways, swinging, transferring weight, pulling, pushing, pressing, falling, swaying, gliding, tapping, striking etc., primarily without locomotion.

Equipment (balls of various kinds, bean bags, hoops, canes and ropes) is particularly useful for giving motivation for exercises.

All the ways of moving outlined above can, of course, be combined with locomotion. In general a travelling movement suits a child's motor needs better than moving on the spot which requires far greater concentration and a more subtle control of the body. Nevertheless, movement on the spot should not be neglected in teaching. Imaginative aids related to the child's realm of experience and the use of equipment and instruments can broaden the expressive capacity and develop technique.

Bending and straightening

General characteristics

Bending is the bringing together of two parts of the body that are linked by a joint (e.g. thigh and shank) through the contraction of the flexor muscles. In straightening, the extensor muscles are contracted, thus separating again the two parts linked by a joint. For work with children the most important possibilities for bending and straightening are:

Head and neck: Bending forwards (chin touches the chest); bending backwards (back of head touches the top of the back); bending sideways (the ear is brought near to the shoulder).

Trunk: In bending forwards, backwards or sideways either the whole of the spine or only the upper part of it can be involved. The spine is most flexible in forward bending.

Arms: Bending and straightening in the finger, wrist and elbow joints.

Legs: Bending and straightening in the toe, ankle, knee and hip joints, in the latter the bending occurs between the trunk and the thigh.

Movement variations: The use of imaginative stimuli (reaching for something, trying to grasp something, carrying something heavy, making oneself tall or small); complete or partial bending and straightening; .asymmetrical or symmetrical movements while lying, sitting, kneeling, squatting or standing.

Summary

Space: Contracting and spreading out the whole body or individual parts of it forwards, backwards and sideways (as far as is functionally possible); while lying, kneeling, sitting and standing.

Bending is generally directed inwards to the body, whilst straightening is directed away from it. The extent of the movement can lead to the most intensive bending and the most extreme straightening, but it can also be kept to a minimum.

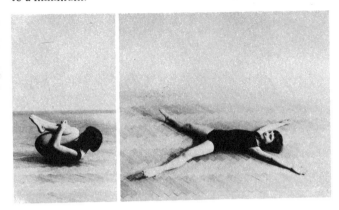

Extreme bending and straightening while lying and standing

Time: Fast or slow; smooth or jerky; increasing or decreasing in tempo; mostly in free rhythm, rarely bound by an accompaniment.

Dynamics: More energy is required in fast or extreme bending than in slow movements of a limited extent. Acquiring control over the expenditure of energy is achieved by setting a great variety of tasks (as far as tempo and the extent of the movement are concerned). Accented movements are possible.

Group formations: Working and playing together, partners helping each other by gentle pushing or pulling to assist the bending and straightening can add variety to this work.

Main faults and corrections

--Movements that are too limited: The extent of the movement can be increased by designing the tasks to this end, e.g. bending the whole body until, in the squatting position, the forehead touches the knees; stretching as high and wide as possible.

Excessive bending or straightening leading to rigidity: This can be overcome by learning to accomplish bending and stretching in succession without holding the breath.

Rotating inwards, outwards and twisting

General characteristics

As distinct from turning the whole body on its axis, discussed previously, rotating inwards and outwards involves the rotation of legs or arms. Rotating inwards means turning towards the body axis, rotating outwards means turning away from it. Twisting means turning the head, shoulders or pelvis over a fixed, supporting base.

Turns of this kind are to some extent a necessary preparation for other kinds of movement (e.g. rotating the legs outwards prepares for cross-over steps, rotating the arms in both directions prepares for swinging in circles and figures of eight and also for sustained arm movements. On the other hand these rotations can be considered as movement possibilities in their own right that should be explored by the children.

Rotating the limbs inwards and outwards   Twisting the head and the trunk

Movement variations: Inward or outward rotation of arms or legs when they are either bent or straight in opposition to circling with hand, foot, forearm or shank; twisting the head sideways; extending this movement through the inclusion of the trunk; use of imaginative stimuli such as rubber or wire puppets, marionettes etc.

Summary

Space: Circling and turning the head, the trunk and the extremities in different directions, in different positions (standing, sitting, kneeling, lying) and levels

(circling the arms above the head, to the side or in front of the body); inward and outward rotation of the legs (in front of, behind and to the side of the body); the compass of the movement extends from small to as large as possible.
Time: Both quick and slow movements are possible. Initially, a slower tempo is recommended, especially for as long as the movements remain unfamiliar. The biggest possible extension of movement is also easier to achieve at first at a slow tempo. More experienced children can attempt free rhythms or changes of tempo that are given in a predetermined accompaniment. It is generally preferable, however, to have either no accompaniment or one that is without metre.
Dynamics: Different degrees of energy expenditure corresponding to the extent and speed of the movement produce a sustained swinging or "torn" performance. In working with apparatus the individual characteristics of any apparatus used dictate the dynamics to a great extent. Thus sustained movements with a rope are rather senseless since this then hangs slackly. Movements associated with work with a ball that are too intense and "torn" are out of the question since they make it impossible to handle the ball.
Group formations: Here group formations depend particularly upon the nature of the task to be solved. Placed facing one another is suitable for mirroring, echo-work, question and answer and contrasting; placed side by side is suitable for symmetrical or parallel work.

Swaying with transfer of weight

General characteristics

Every swinging movement consists of three phases: the up beat of breathing in, the yielding to gravity in a falling movement and the overcoming of gravity in a rising movement. The resulting curve is an arc that can be extended into a circle or a figure of eight. If we think of the action of a pendulum each swing can fade out when no fresh impulse follows the initial one. A small amount of energy is sufficient to sustain the swinging motion if the extent of the rising and falling movements are equal. The swing can also be developed by constantly increasing the impulses, until the arc-shaped movement eventually becomes a circle.

Here we shall mainly discuss the transfer of weight through a swaying movement and simple pendulum swinging for the following reasons: children in the age group under consideration generally lack the body weight, the bulk and the sensitivity that are necessary for big swings of the whole body. These large body swings are undoubtedly valuable gymnastic exercises but they do not belong to the elemental dance material which is used in traditional dances.
Swinging: This is a movement of the whole body though different parts of the body can take over the pendulum movement.
Head: Swings in a semicircle from side to side; swings round in a circle from one side over the other back to the starting position.
Arms: Parallel or contrary motion; pendulum swings forwards/backwards near the body, high/low or in front of the body from the outside inwards (the whole

body—particularly its centre of gravity—swings with the movement, with the necessary give in ankle, knee and hip joints). Swings in a circle or figure of eight that are performed in front, beside or above the body are more difficult. They are generally more appropriately introduced after puberty and best executed with the help of equipment (bean bags, balls, hoops or ropes). Swinging in a circle can be started inwards (towards the body) or outwards (away from the body).

Pendulum arm swinging with the youngest age group

Trunk: High/low pendulum swing (see arm swinging) up to a fully upright position of the body; a sideways pendulum swing with feet apart. The trunk cannot, of course, swing in isolation. Every impulse dies away in a movement of the head and arms, while the legs give at the joints to a greater or lesser degree according to the energy of the impulse.

Legs: Pendulum swing forwards/backwards or outwards/inwards; swinging in a circle in front of or behind the body, in a figure of eight alternately in front of and behind the supporting leg.

Leg swing with partner's help

Transfer of weight through swaying: This should be practised with feet together, with one foot slightly in front of the other when it can lead to locomotion forwards or backwards, or with feet apart, the body weight then being shifted sideways in a succession of side and close steps or crossing steps in front of or behind the supporting leg. With experienced children the locomotion can be extended and combined with intermediate steps and whole or half turns. Transfer of weight through swaying with feet together: The body is upright, the weight equally distributed between both feet. The weight is then carefully shifted forwards (onto the balls of the feet and the toes) without lifting the heels from the floor, and then brought back to the original position. The weight is then shifted backwards (owing to the anatomy of the foot swaying backwards is more limited) and back again to the centre. The soles of both feet always remain in contact with the floor and the weight rests alternately on the balls of the feet and on the heels. The transfer of weight should not be so pronounced as to upset the balance and the body should not bend at the hips.

By turning the leg slightly out from the hips the weight can be shifted sideways from one foot to the other. The heels remain touching and both feet remain in contact with the floor. A certain degree of muscular control is a prerequisite for both these exercises and they develop and encourage a sensitive feeling for balance. To improve concentration it is a good idea to practise them with the eyes closed.

Transfer of weight through swaying with feet apart: The weight of the body, focussed in the pelvis, is shifted in an inverted arc from side to side in the horizontal plane. The supporting leg bends; the weight is then transferred until it is evenly distributed between both, slightly bent, legs; as the weight is transferred to the new supporting leg, this leg bends more and the free leg is straightened. During this movement the body's weight should at no time rest on the inner side of the feet but should be placed evenly between the balls of the feet and the heels. To avoid sagging at the knees care should be taken that while they are bent the knees remain in a direct line over the toes.

Transfer of weight through swaying with one foot slightly in front of the other: As above, this movement describes an inverted arc in the horizontal plane. The supporting leg bends; the weight is then transferred forwards or backwards until it is evenly distributed between both, slightly bent, legs; as the weight is transferred to the new supporting leg, this leg bends more and the free leg is straightened.

The transfer of weight sideways or forwards or backwards can be repeated in the opposite direction so that a continuous right and left or forwards and backwards movement ensues.

Movement variations: The different effects that energy and tempo have upon swinging movements should be tried out extensively with and without equipment. Progression from swaying with weight transference to swinging locomotion or turning should be tried.

Summary

Space; Directions of swing are forwards/backwards, right/left, high/low or turning; the movement can be done on the spot or travelling; the centre of gravity moves during the swing; the extent of the swing varies from very small to very large.

Time: Every swing and every transfer of weight requires a certain time that is in relation to the size and weight of the body. A fast movement will be smaller, a slow one larger. Considering the physical differences found in a class it is advisable to practise these movements at individual speeds and without accompaniment at first. The adaptation to a musical accompaniment can follow later (rhythms and melodies in a swinging time like three-four, six-eight and nine-eight are especially suitable).

Dynamics: With equal expenditure of energy the extent of the movement remains constant; if the impetus is increased the movement becomes larger and more intense, eventually leading to locomotion. If the energy is reduced the movement becomes smaller, fades away and eventually reaches stillness.

Group formations: Practising with a partner and using equipment (passing balls or small bean bags in a swinging movement) develops adaptation to the equipment and to the partner. In forming pairs or small groups height and weight should be taken into consideration; where these do not match a common swinging movement will only be possible through acceleration or slowing down of individual tempi, if at all. Holding by the hand is not at all suitable for swinging and only rarely for the transfer of weight through swaying.

Main faults and corrections

—Arm swinging with stiff legs: This means simply that a peripheral pendulum movement of the arms is being made. The children should try to bring the arms into a swing motivated from the knees. Working with balls or bean bags that are not too light requires a more intensive drive from the knees.

—"Snatching" instead of swinging: Tempo and extent of the swing do not match one another. The swing must be made smaller or the tempo slower. Equipment held in the hand will help to produce a more appropriate use of energy.

104

—Directing the movement instead of swinging: Here too there is a divergence between the extent of the movement and the tempo, but this has gone to the opposite extreme. The tempo must be increased or the movement made larger. Direction means here a movement that is continuously active without the moment of passive fall that is characteristic of the swing.

—Stiff back and neck: The swing normally starts as an undulation through the spine. With a tense posture this is impossible. In this case the movement is halting and appears stiff. It is often sufficient to let the head hang loosely to release the tension of the spine. In difficult cases special exercises for relieving tension are needed.

Pushing, pulling, pressing, spreading, contracting, falling and rolling

These and many more ways of moving can be practised on their own account or in connection with travelling movements. They can all be tried out and varied according to the aspects already discussed and with the help of imaginative stimuli. Individual descriptions of all these possibilities would be far beyond the compass of the present book.

Movement combinations

Once the children are conversant with the basic movements they can embark upon the wide field of movement combinations. These prepare and distinguish the possibilities for expression in dance and set the children new standards of learning and creating.

"Movement combinations" can be described as follows:

A succession of individual movements, e.g. running forwards, bouncing on the spot, running backwards.

Synchronisation of two or more ways of moving, e.g. running with a swing, turning while skipping.

Both kinds should be practised with the children, but the succession of individual movements is generally easier than the synchronisation. It is advisable to allow the children to practise a change between two ways of moving (e.g. running and skipping) first for themselves, therefore without accompaniment and also without any particular phrase structure. The task can so be set that they only try to change as often as is possible. In this way each child will work according to his own level of ability.

Once the transition from one movement to another within a framework of free change is under control, then an accompaniment that gives a phrasing that is valid for everyone can be used; at first in longer phrases (i.e. eight bars). As the capacity to react quickly increases these phrases can become shorter—four bars, two or even one bar in length.

Once the change offers no more difficulties, then spatial considerations can be introduced (changes of direction, particular movement paths, linking up in groups of two or more). The sequence should never appear constructed, but should allow for a flowing, natural movement.

The following are a few examples of the almost unlimited possibilities for combination and should stimulate individual solutions.

Walking with a final step and close:
In order to end a phrase of walking either forwards or backwards clearly, the working leg is placed next to the supporting leg on the last step. This produces a conclusion or a return to the original position. This conclusion should be supported in the accompaniment through clear phrase endings (e.g. a longer note value).

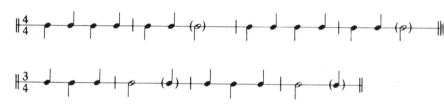

If the movement has formerly been carried out in one direction, this can be changed from forwards to backwards after a while, the change possibly being emphasised with a clap.
Variations: For the closing-up step the working leg can be placed beside the supporting leg either silently or with a stamp using the whole foot, the ball or the heel.

Walking or running, jumping the feet together to finish:
This is in place of the step and close in the previous exercises. According to the rhythmic structure the jump closing the feet is either a large one or small and quick.

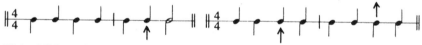

With children that are more skilled the jump can be combined with a quarter turn, half turn (example given in notation) or whole turn.

After the jump with a half turn the walking starts backwards.

Various means of locomotion with sound gestures:
The inclusion of sound gestures (clapping, patschen, finger-snapping and

106

stamping) in combination with walking, and also with skipping or running, provides a wide variety of rhythmic movement variations that can be simplified or made more difficult according to the age or ability of the children concerned.

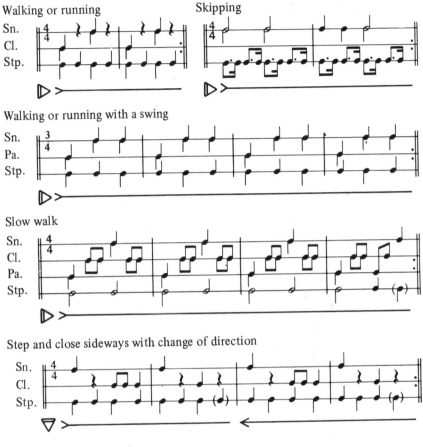

Walking or running   Skipping

Sn.
Cl.
Stp.

Walking or running with a swing

Sn.
Pa.
Stp.

Slow walk

Sn.
Cl.
Pa.
Stp.

Step and close sideways with change of direction

Sn.
Cl.
Stp.

Walking with occasional stamps:
    A stamp that is used as the conclusion to a sequence of steps is often to be found in Slavonic, Spanish and other folk dances.

The stamp as a conclusion to a sequence of steps

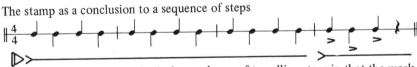

Stamps can also be made during a phrase of travelling steps in that the working foot touches the floor either lightly or with tension with the ball of the foot, the heel or the whole foot. The weight does not have to be transferred on every stamp.

Stamps made while travelling

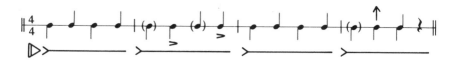

Walking and stamping with a jump that lands with feet together

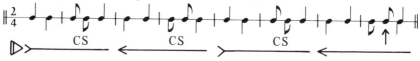

Variation: The stamp is not made directly into the floor but rather "brushes" the floor in a forward direction or from the outside inwards.

Combinations with change-steps:
    This change-step develops out of stepping or stamping lightly on the spot (in the rhythm: quaver-quaver-crotchet).

Change steps when walking forwards and backwards

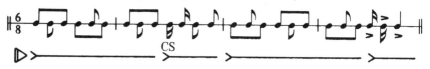

Change steps in a swinging run (large curves on the floor)

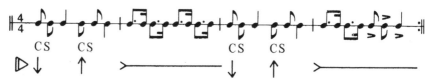

Change steps sideways with skipping forwards

Walking and skipping:
    Most children find this combination very easy. In the transition from skipping to walking the forward drive of energy has to be controlled in order to avoid falling into the first walking step.

108

Skipping forwards and walking backwards

Walking forwards and skipping with a turn

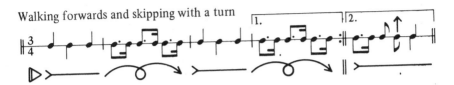

Sideways step and close with change of direction:

Simple change of direction with slow and fast steps

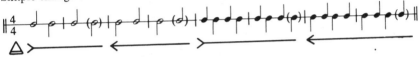

Change of direction with stamps

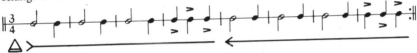

Half turns with constant direction in pairs

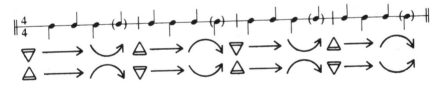

(The partner always uses the opposite leg)

Sideways cross-over step:

Sideways cross-over step with bouncing and finger-snapping on the spot. (out=stepping out sideways; bef.=working leg crosses in front of supporting leg; beh.=working leg crosses behind; tog.=closing working leg to supporting leg)

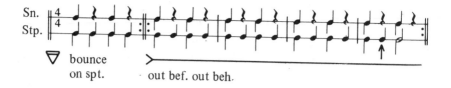

Sn.
Stp.

bounce on spt.   out bef. out beh.

Cross-over step from side to side with swinging walk forwards

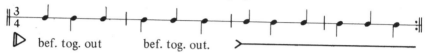

bef. tog. out   bef. tog. out.

Changing between small, double bounce steps and wide, walked cross-over steps with change of direction.

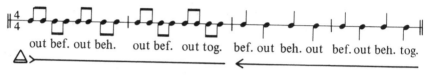

out bef. out beh.   out bef.   out tog.   bef. out beh. out   bef. out beh. tog.

When bouncing the body is lifted, the arms held high. When stepping wide the trunk and knees are bent, the focus of movement rather low; the arms are held low and swing forwards and backwards (when in circle or chain formation).

Running and skipping;

Running forwards (or backwards), turning on the spot with bouncing (on one leg)

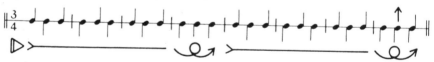

Skipping with intermediate steps and change of direction

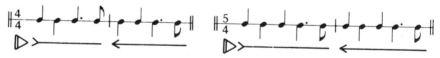

Running and skipping steps in zigzag, change of direction every three bars

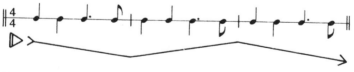

110

Bouncing and skipping:

Simple bouncing run forwards, skipping backwards

Double bounce forwards, skipping forwards with a turn

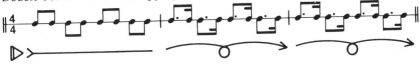

Double bounce sideways and skipping forwards, simple bounce on the spot

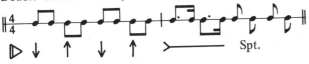

Running and jumping:

Run and leap or gallop jump

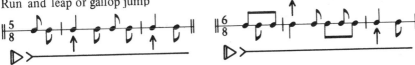

The steps for the preparatory run are on the weak beat, the main accent comes on the take-off for the jump. The run can be combined with a leap (straight legs) or with a gallop jump (bent legs).

Running with turning jump

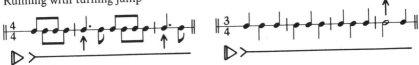

Transfer of weight through swaying on the spot and in locomotion:

Transfer of weight with locomotion

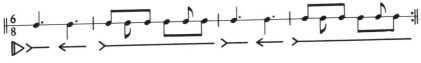

Sideways transfer of weight with a turn

Bending and stretching:
   The children change between stretching and bending their whole body through a metrically free accompaniment of individual "signals" on cymbal and gong.
Changes of tempo: slow bending--fast stretching.
Increase of tempo: Beginning with slow bending and stretching the movement becomes ever smaller and faster.

Arm and leg gestures:
   Small or large circles are drawn in the air or on the ground alternately with one or both arms or with one foot. These movements can also be combined with walking.

The setting of tasks that give experience of the concepts of time, dynamics, space, and form

The previous section of this book has dealt with different ways of moving and their variations, many faults and their corrections.

The material in this chapter is organised from a different point of view. Concepts of time, dynamics, space and form should be experienced and tried out with the help of the movement material already outlined. This occurs in exercises that are variable and that take the form of games, not yet in fixed dance forms and movement sequences. Examples in the setting of such tasks should clarify this.

In order to arrange the material clearly it has been divided into four areas or themes—some overlapping is inevitable.

Setting tasks in the realm of "time"

Through these exercises the children should experience and learn to understand those aspects of time that affect music and dance: tempo, i.e. slow and fast, changing gradually or suddenly; beginning, duration and end of a musical or movement sequence, i.e. entry, phrasing and cadence. Rests and rhythmic motifs, different metres, the simplest forms of one and two-part work.

Exercises in time
--Contrasts between fast and slow: each child shows two extremes of speed. He can imagine the difference between the movements of an old man and those of a high-spirited child, between the speed of a horse and cart and a racing car, or he can work without any particular picture in his imagination. These experiments can make use of walking and running, but also of creeping and rolling on the floor or of other similar, unconventional means of locomotion. One should not forget that it is also possible to work with arms, head or trunk and to find a way of moving slowly or quickly that does not involve locomotion and that can be executed while lying, sitting, kneeling or standing.
--Accelerando and ritardando in movement and accompaniment: In a group the children practise gradual changes of tempo. With small children this is more successful when in the form of a game. Several children stand one behind the other and form a train. It starts to move slowly, gets faster and faster; when it approaches a station it slows down until it finally stops. If the group is a

large one two or more groups can be made. Train number one starts first, perhaps a goods train that cannot travel so very fast. Once it has arrived at a station the express train starts, etc. Attention could be paid to the spatial factor during this game in that the first child (the locomotive) leads along a particular path (a circle, along the walls, zigzag, in curves). The children's imagination will help to elaborate this game. Perhaps one group could accompany the "driving" of the trains by clapping the pulse or beat.

—Reaction to a tempo given in an accompaniment: The teacher accompanies very softly in a steady tempo while the children listen with closed eyes. Once they have the feel of the tempo they tap their knees or clap quietly in time. Finally, with their eyes open, they start moving to the accompaniment. This exercise will give rise mainly to locomotion. Each child can walk or run on his own, or pairs, small groups, a chain or a circle can be formed. As an exception one could ask the children to respond in time but without moving their legs so that their arm and trunk movements would be more stimulated. After a short time a change of tempo is introduced. The same procedure is followed: listen—accompany—move. Some children find it difficult at first to adapt their own tempo to the accompaniment of a tambour, bongos or recorder. There are some ways of getting over this difficulty.

—Pre-school age children can sing a song that is well-known to them and while doing so they hold hands and walk round in a circle. In most cases the tempo of the song immediately determines the tempo of the movement.

—The teacher accompanies the children's walking, running and skipping. The accompaniment changes according to the movement (but the children always clap continuous crotchets). Walking is most suitably accompanied with crotchets, running with quavers (the crotchet beat here being slightly slower than for walking) and skipping with a crotchet-quaver rhythm in six-eight time.

—A slow tempo is more difficult the younger the children are. Arranging the task so that the time can be filled out more easily has proved helpful. "Walking, lifting the knee high between each step" is far easier than "walking very slowly". Clapping, singing or speaking is added.

Working at the beginning and end of a movement

Once the difficulties of "keeping the tempo" and "changing the tempo" have been overcome, starting and finishing together needs to be practised. With small children one does not initially stress the importance of starting all together. They have to acclimatise themselves to so much that is new that details can be overlooked for the present. There comes a time, however, when everyone should begin together and with the accompaniment. One can assist this through the use of words. The names of the children in the group can be used, or a simple text that calls upon them to begin.

Pe— ter, Ti— mo— thy, Pa— tri-- cia and Sa— man-- tha, are you there? are you rea-dy This is when we start.

—The start is practised at first without movement. The teacher plays the rhythm of the text, the children listen, or can straight away speak it with her, and indicate the start of the movement by clapping on the first beat of the following bar. Later the start of the movement can be indicated by an accented step. Another stage is reached when the children can start exactly together after only listening to the introduction while it is played. Once the start has become quite secure with the help of words and introduction one can dispense with both. The teacher now only needs to give the signal to start with her "up-beat" intake of breath.

This preparation through breathing in is important for every group entry when speaking, singing, clapping, playing instruments or moving and especially when dancing. It is a short "up-beat" intake of breath that is relative to the tempo that is to follow. (Take special care that the shoulders are not raised with the intake of breath.)

The children should very soon try taking the place of the teacher and giving the starting signal.

Finishing together is as important as starting together in all group work. A well-known song (e.g. "Here we go round the mulberry bush" or something else suitable for older children) will again give help here.

—At first the children and the teacher sing together paying attention to the words and the melodic shape of the end of the song. Then they move to the melody (the kind of movements they make should naturally be related to the tempo and character of the song). They should find a clear ending to their movement that coincides with the end of the melody.

—Reaction exercise: The teacher or a child accompanies walking, running, skipping. At a predetermined signal (the accompaniment stops, a strong accent or a call) the children stop suddenly.

—Prepared ending to a longer movement sequence: Again some preparatory work is done with words, at first without movement while standing or sitting. The children take notice of when the teacher says (rhythmically): "Now you stop!" On the word "stop" they should clap.

—Now they try to find the "stop" in the movement. All run freely about the room listening attentively to the accompaniment. On the word "stop" they jump their feet together and remain standing without losing their balance. After a while the teacher drops the words, but in her accompaniment accents the ending so clearly that it acts as an acoustic signal to the children.

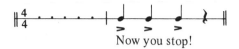

Now you stop!

Working out different phrasings

When the children have understood the beginning and ending of a movement they must learn about the duration of a phrase, so that the teacher no longer needs to bring sequences to an end with a signal. We are now familiar with using words and must look for a song the children know, e.g. "What shall we do with the drunken sailor? "

—This is sung and accompanied with patschen and clapping. Later, two groups stand opposite one another, one accompanying and the other skipping to it in a chain behind a leader. On the word "morning" the end of the phrase is marked by the children jumping their feet together. The groups exchange activities. At the same time various tasks concerned with the use of space can be set: skipping forwards and backwards, in a circle, in curves.

—The next stage is for every child to have a turn alone. All stand in a circle and one after the other each dances the phrase alone, returning to his original place by the end of the phrase. It is particularly important that there should be no waiting between one entry and the next. As soon as one child has finished the next one begins, and so on, round the circle, one after the other.

—This can later be developed by singing the words very softly, then only thinking them through. Finally the phrase of sixteen beats can be felt naturally and taken for granted. Longer, or irregular phrases can also be studied in this way.

Working out rests

This should include both the individual rests that occur within a text, song or piece of music as well as longer rests of one or more bars.

—In principal the children should experience that a rest is not a void or vacuum but a period of stillness. With children of nursery school age it is possible to fill out a rest that occurs in speaking or singing by making a gesture indicating silence (laying a finger on the lips). While doing this the children should listen very carefully to see whether there really is absolute stillness.

—All children walk in a circle, speaking and clapping a sequence of names of those present. In the rest (e.g. after a name with one syllable) a moment of concentrated listening occurs. The gestures serve as an introduction to the idea and can soon be left out.

Ma -- ry,   Su -- san,   Da -- vid,   Paul.

—With slightly older children the rest can be expressed as a silent "beat" in the air. As a variation in locomotion the free leg taps the ground silently with the toes during the rest.

—Working at longer rests: For this a proverb can be used.

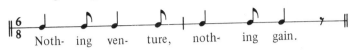

Noth- ing ven- ture, noth- ing gain.

—At first the text is spoken, or possibly sung to a melody that the children make up. To this the children then improvise simple dance steps within the meaning of the words. First the text is heard as they dance, then each child thinks through the words but moves as before. Next, the movement is also left out and intense concentration is directed onto thinking the words through. The new movement entry must be precise. A rest should never be a vacuum. The listening for something inaudible—the suspense—must be maintained.

In this way one can practise rests that last for a complete phrase. Later, shorter texts can be used where rests of only one bar occur. The teacher must take care that every new entry is prepared for with an intake of breath, and that phrasing is clear. Her demonstration of this should be clear and convincing.

Working at different kinds of time
—Familiar songs in two-four or four-four time are sung. The children provide a rhythmic accompaniment in which only the first beat, the strongest rhythmic accent, is clapped. After a while the weaker beats are also included. Through giving them different sounds the strong and weak beats in a bar can be clearly distinguished from one another. Later, songs in three-four time are added. Accompaniments can be:

Sn.
Cl.
Pa.
St.

—The children now move and sing and indicate the strong beats with an accentuated step on the floor. They can fulfil tasks of this kind long before they know what a three-four or a four-four bar is.

As soon as the children can understand, with the help of known melodies and texts, and can show in performance the difference between accented and unaccented, between strong and weak, a reaction to exclusively rhythmic accompaniments or to unknown melodies will be possible.

—The teacher plays a rhythm in two-four time on a drum and the children emphasise the accents in their movement. For this they can walk or run forwards, and later on backwards. Different movement paths and group formations are also possible.

—A melody in three-four time is played on a recorder by the teacher or another child. When the steps are regular the accent comes on alternate feet. The entire sole should be used for the accentuated step, the balls of the feet for the unaccented.

—This exercise can be practised in every kind of time. The children walk
forwards, and later backwards or sideways in a circle, the steps coinciding
with the pulse beat. Simple rhythms are then clapped over these beats, at first
as an echo or imitation exercise, later as question and answer (see p. 130). A
child can soon take the place of the teacher and give the questions, the others
taking it in turns to invent answers.

—To the accompaniment of the teacher (recorder, singing) the children try to
find movements that correspond to the time signature and that also fit the
melody: march-like walking; polka-step etc. for two-four time; swinging walk,
running and three-four time.

Once specific kinds of time are familiar to the children, both musically and in
movement, then time-changes can be introduced.

—The change of time is prepared with the help of words or a melody.

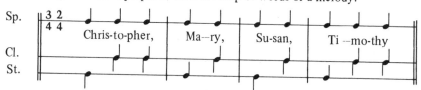

At first the names are spoken and clapped. Soon one can omit the words and
the first beat of each bar is stamped. Finally one movement for the three-four
bars and another for the two-four can be tried. The most suitable examples are
chosen from the children's individual solutions. Two differing possibilities are:

—Changing between forwards running steps and double bounce on the spot.

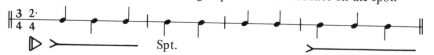

—Moving sideways: Changing between stamping and step and close

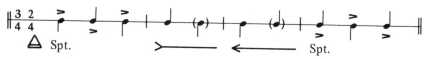

Working out rhythmic motifs

Rhythmic motifs are introduced through names and word series that have a
common subject matter suggested by the children. They are practised as exercises
in echoing or question and answer with the inclusion of sound gestures (stamping,
patschen, clapping and finger-snapping) and step patterns. If the children know
French time names from their music lessons then they can also be included. When
the rhythms have become familiar and natural the words can be left out. Simple
rhythms can be repeated (as ostinati) on the spot and in locomotion. They can
serve later as "building bricks" for simple forms.

—Simple alternation between stamping and finger-snapping: each stamp can
lead either forwards, backwards or sideways. The snapping can follow with

118

the arms held high over the head, or with arms held parallel in front of the body, or to the right and left. The arm movement should flow and be in time. (Ostinato 1)

—Down-beat and up-beat are stamped, giving the sequence an onward drive. (Ostinato 2)

—Two-bar ostinato in three-four time: First practised on the spot being careful to maintain a gentle, flowing movement in the arms. Then locomotion can be tried (walking or swinging run) with additional changes of direction, straight and curved paths or in pairs. (Ostinato 3)

—Two-bar ostinato in two-four time: The stamps are evenly-spaced and are therefore most suitable for locomotion. To help the rhythm words can be used at first. Perhaps: "Practice makes perfect" or something similar. (Ostinato 4)

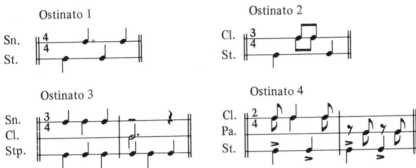

Certain rhythmic motifs are a characteristic of individual types of movement or combinations of steps (Pavane, Sarabande, Galliard or in the realm of the newer social dances: Tango or Cha-Cha-Cha). For our material this applies particularly to the skipping and change step rhythms. Children very quickly associate such rhythms with particular movements, but this is not to say that no other kinds of movements to these rhythms are allowed.

—Four types of movement with their corresponding accompaniments are available for choice: Walking, running, skipping and change step. To this the teacher or a child plays one of the following accompaniments:

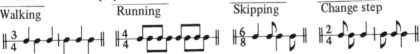

The children listen to the accompaniment, clap it quietly and then move to it freely round the room or on predetermined movement paths, alone or in pairs, in small groups or in given formations. They can be divided into four groups, each group taking one type of movement and having its own particular accompanying instrument (tambour, finger cymbals, claves and sleigh bells). Each group moves only when its instrument sounds. The change from one instrument to another can be regular or unexpected. If two instruments are played simultaneously then two groups should be moving.

Rhythmic work in two parts

The initial introduction to rhythmic work in two parts can be to bring to the children's attention two different sounds that can be heard simultaneously (sound of an approaching car and the horn of another car; a ticking clock and the sound of a man breathing; footsteps of children in the room and the teacher's voice). The children should find similar examples themselves. Finally, one can create such simultaneous sounds, at first without rhythmic organisation (one child with his feet, another with his hands), then in a rhythmically organised form, perhaps with the help of the ostinati previously practised. Two children or two groups each take an ostinato and perform it in sound gestures and movement, the others watch and listen.

—Some children form an inner circle and snap the first ostinato (given below) while stepping evenly forwards, backwards or sideways (facing centre). Other children form an outer circle and, walking in the same tempo but in the opposite direction, they clap the second ostinato. Each group should listen carefully to the other. After a certain time (e.g. after 16, 8 or 4 bars) they exchange ostinati. Variety can be introduced by means of other rhythms, other types of movement or other movement paths.

Ostinato 1   Ostinato 2

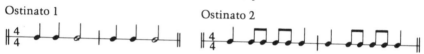

In the following example there are no longer two ostinati sounding simultaneously, but a continuous, improvised or predetermined rhythm that is performed over the accompaniment of an ostinato.

—Group 1 takes the ostinato, Group 2 the continuous rhythm. To this a simple space form is added. Group 1 stands in a circle, the ostinato is stamped and clapped and at every new bar a quarter turn is made. Group 2 forms a chain behind a leader and walks in and out of those in the circle.

Introduction

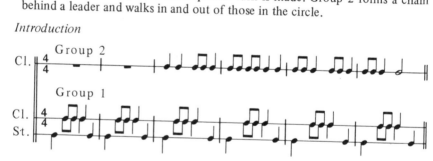

Formation

120

Setting tasks in the realm of "dynamics"

Through the following examples, the children's attention should be drawn and their sensitivity awakened to the dynamic aspects of movement. In speaking, singing, playing instruments and in dancing they should learn to express different levels of intensity as various degrees of tension, continuous or sudden in transition, regular or irregular in accentuation.

Preparatory exercises for aural training
—What loud or quiet sounds do they know? Quiet — a cat, a balloon, raindrops, a pocket watch; loud — thunder, an explosion, a jet engine starting. The children will find many other examples.
—The children can make loud and soft noises themselves with their voices, with their hands or feet: whispering and screaming, tiptoeing silently and stamping loudly, clapping softly with fingers only and clapping heavily with cupped hands.
—The whole group walks (runs, skips, bounces). One child sits in the middle of the room with closed eyes. The remaining children all move together, or only some of them move while the others watch. The child in the middle tries to guess how many are moving.
—The children sit spaced out in the room with eyes closed. One child moves as quietly as possible among them. Through the sound that his feet make the children should be aware of whether he is far or near to them and in which part of the room he is at any given time.
—All the children sit in a circle, their hands over their eyes. One child stamps, claps his hands together or on the floor, snaps or does patschen in the centre. The others must recognise the sound and say whether it was loud or soft.

Reaction and concentration exercises with dynamic stimuli
At first only two contrasting levels of sound are used; once the reaction to these is sure, more can be introduced.
—The children move freely and without accompaniment around the room. At a soft beat on a tambour they should immediately stand still; if they hear a loud beat they should, quick as lightening, lie on the floor; with a medium loud one they should stand on one leg (balancing exercise).
—One group moves when the accompaniment is soft, the other when it is loud. The change from one to the other should be fairly quick since the aim is to train their quick reaction.
—While the children are moving, one of them strikes a cymbal. The others remain standing and listening for as long as they can still hear the sound of the cymbal. Only when the sound has quite died away do they resume their movement again.
—Again the cymbal is struck. While the sound reverberates the children make themselves small and sink slowly to the floor. When they can hear nothing

more they lie still. When the sound is made once more they rise carefully. They reach a fully upright standing position only when the sound has completely died away. This task is not so simple for small children. They have difficulty in moving slowly, in "distributing" their movement as it were.

Through exercises of this kind concepts such as forte, piano, crescendo, and decrescendo become clear. After a while they are given their appropriate names and symbols.

It is not sufficient, however, only to be able to recognise and understand dynamic differences, but one must also be able to perform them. In movement soft and loud imply less or more tension. A movement may only be "loud" in exceptional circumstances.

—The accompaniment changes between soft and loud: the children try, by stamping on the whole foot and walking on the balls of the feet, to find a movement to match the accompaniment. In doing this it is not the loudness of the stamping, but the degree of tension in the body that is important.

—All the children start clapping quietly together — the clapping becomes louder and louder as if a crowd was slowly approaching. (Crescendo exercise, the same idea in reverse for decrescendo. The teacher must take care that the crescendos do not get faster nor the decrescendos slower.)

—Half the children accompany with their hands or on instruments; they make a crescendo that starts pianissimo and increases to forte. The other children try to express this crescendo (in movement). They very soon realise that the increase of energy can express itself through a more intensive use of space. They begin with quiet, small steps and finish at the forte with long, vigorous, almost leaping steps.

—The teacher plays on a drum, sometimes very softly, then crescendo, with sudden accents, decrescendo etc. The children try to match their movements to the changing dynamics. They soon notice that, according to the accompaniment, their gestures and steps need to be sometimes sharp and accented, then again small and economical, and that more energy and tension are required for crescendo and less for decrescendo. Exercises of this kind should be practised in locomotion as well as on the spot. For the one the emphasis will be laid on steps, jumps and turns, for the other on the movement of the trunk, arms and hands, neck and head. Imaginative stimuli can be helpful in some cases.

—Changing accents are practised: The accents should not be particularly loud, but the other notes should rather be quieter. Then the children try to find accents in movement, for instance: stamping while walking, changing direction, a small jump, pushing arm movements and so on.

The younger the children are the shorter the rhythmic phrases with which they work must be, otherwise their capacity for memory and concentration will be overtaxed. For this kind of exercise a nonsense rhyme might be used, individual words of which are suddenly called out loudly or whispered quietly.

This idea with words can be transferred onto instruments or into movement and repeated or varied.

Most of the examples already given have asked for a movement response to an accompaniment that contains a variety of dynamic levels. The children should also be stimulated to try out small movement sequences containing dynamic variety for themselves. Ideas can be motivated by talking to the children (e.g. the representation of a particularly strong character from the children's reading matter such as Asterix both with and without the magic potion, or the wind that blows with different degrees of intensity, or some object that is being blown by the wind).

—Each child sits on the floor and tries to make sounds with hands and feet. He can also try with finger-tips, knuckles, flat palms, back of the hands, fist, heels, balls of the feet, toes or sole. In this exercise it is not the rhythm or tempo that is important but rather the imaginative and dynamic play with these simple sound effects. Some children can demonstrate their results to the others.

—Spaced out round the room, each child works alone. With steps, stamping, clapping, little jumps or arm gestures he tries, starting quite softly, to become louder and louder and to finish with a particularly strong movement.

—This exercise is similar to the previous one, but instead of a continuous crescendo he should try a freely changing pattern of loud and soft. Since over-emphasised stamping is harmful and because the children should learn that it is not "loudness" but physical tension that is important, one can gradually make it clear that the loud movements should be seen but not heard. The movements will soon acquire more tension and intensity in their use of space. The children themselves should judge whether a movement is visibly "loud" or "soft". Finally instead of "loud" and "soft" the terms "strong" and "weak", "energetic" and "delicate" can be used.

Setting tasks in the realm of "space"

As we know from experience, the nature of the space in which children are to move greatly influences the movement itself. A classroom with forms or tables demands different ways of negotiating space from a gymnasium. A school playground or a lawn offers different spatial stimuli from an enclosed music room.

Orientation, spacing out, making use of large areas, movement paths and directions, group formations and the ways of holding that are related to them; these form the subject matter of the following exercises.

Orientation exercises
—The children must first explore the room in which the lesson is to take place. To do this they run freely about the whole room or hall. They go into all the

corners, move diagonally, in zigzags and along the walls. They run in curved lines, circles, figures of eight, spirals, just as the spirit moves them. They can romp about, trip along daintily or take big leaps. Some run alone, others move in twos or in small groups.

This experimenting provides the raw material that will be differentiated through the setting of tasks, through working with obstacles in the room, through examples shown by child or teacher, through working with partners or in groups. Movement accompaniment can be added, but not everything needs to be accompanied and the children should learn to listen to the sounds made by their own feet.

Accommodation exercises

—The children walk freely round the room. The only rule: No bumping into walls or other children (first example of accommodating their own movement path to those of others).

—All walk in a group or in a chain, one child leading. In response to a call the leader changes. It is the leader's responsibility to see that the group does not bump into walls and that clear, intelligible movement paths are adopted. The others learn how to adapt and fit into a group.

—Two or more groups move — possibly in different ways — simultaneously about the room. They must not collide and should distribute themselves within the space in the best possible way.

—All the children stand well spaced about the room. They run about to the accompaniment of a drum and stop at a predetermined signal. Everyone now looks to see if there is any part of the room where they are too close together so that large areas are not being used; whether the edge and the centre have been equally well utilised. They will pay more attention to even spacing during the next run.

Working with space on the spot

It is not only walking, running and jumping that lead to spatial awareness but also the use of body position in space. There are the additional possibilities of moving head, trunk, arms and legs in different directions. The relevant exercises can be done kneeling or sitting just as easily as standing. They develop flexibility and movement sensitivity of the trunk and limbs.

—Every child stands on his spot: Where is in front, where is above or to the right? Look in that direction, or indicate it with the whole body or with the hands, legs, head or arms.

—On one occasion work only with the hands. Reach out forwards or backwards, up or down, to the right or the left. Playfully, they can move simultaneously or alternately, in parallel or contrary motion, slowly or fast. Imaginative stimuli (picking flowers or fruit, gathering small objects together, moving the hands like butterflies or small birds) can be used, particularly when these ideas have come from the children themselves.

The hands tell a story

—The legs can explore the space. The toes of the working leg can investigate the floor around the supporting leg. Curved and zigzag lines can be traced on the ground or in the air with heel or toes.

—The body can take up different positions in space: It can make itself tall and narrow (almost like a tower) or small and round (like a ball). It can make a bridge under which a ball can be rolled or someone might even crawl. One can also try to stand broad and tall like a poster board. (The imitation and miming of various animals or objects and their typical movements might also be mentioned here as aids to the imagination.)

Various positions of
the body in space:
tall, round, angular,
broad, narrow

—The transition from one position to the other, and the movements of the hands, arms and legs as well as the trunk can be tried out suddenly and jerkily or evenly and flowing (quasi legato) with much or little tension and at different speeds.

Reaction and concentration exercises

—Arranging themselves in different group formations: In response to a call or to a predetermined acoustic signal (drum beat, end of a melodic phrase) all the children form a circle. Is the circle really in the middle of the room? Is it round? Just as quickly another geometrical form or grouping, chosen by the children, can be made: a semi-circle, a row (facing the teacher, the window or a second row), a chain or a group of three. Two groups should make concentric circles. The announcing of the new formation can come from the children or the teacher and it can be sketched on the blackboard or called out.

—Change of direction as a reaction exercise: All the children walk about the room independently. It is agreed that the accompaniment on the high-pitched drum means "walk forwards" and that on the low-pitched drum means "walk backwards". At first the change is made at fairly long intervals that later become shorter and shorter. The teacher should make sure that the children do not make the change jerkily, but that they achieve a smooth transition.

—Instead of "forwards" and "backwards", "to the right" and "to the left" and, less often, "upwards" and "downwards" are substituted. The latter occurs exclusively on the spot, the others optionally. After some time combinations of changes between three different directions are attempted. It is expedient to practise this first at a slow and then at a faster speed (i.e. first walking and then running or skipping).

When the children have already acquired some skill in dealing with such tasks, then similar ones can also be tried in groups. The examples given so far promote confidence and orientation in space, mainly through visual experience. The following exercises, that should be attempted with eyes closed, strengthen space awareness and train acoustic and tactile perception. Moreover these so-called "blind exercises" are excellent practice in concentration.

—Who can walk in a straight line with eyes closed — without blinking? (Not too many at a time.) As soon as the fear of bumping into someone and the fear of the room that has become strange has disappeared, variations can be added.

—Several children, working alone and with their eyes closed, walk in a small circle, a square, a figure of eight. Nearly all the paths familiar to children can be practised with closed eyes, forwards or backwards. The precondition is that the children have no anxiety. Under no circumstances should they be forced into this. Quiet in the whole room, which also applies to those watching, increases concentration.

—Some children walk about the room and touch all the objects they can reach. This is to ascertain where they are (by the blackboard, near the cupboards, the windows or the instruments).

—Two children work together. One with eyes open leads the other whose eyes are closed. The passive child must remember the path along which he is led so that he can repeat it later with his eyes open.

—Who can find the centre of a circle with eyes closed? When all the children have formed a circle one child, his eyes closed, walks forwards until he thinks he has reached the centre.

—The children join hands (in a circle) and walk with their eyes open to the centre. From this rather haphazard grouping they walk backwards with small steps and with their eyes closed until their arms are stretched. The result is a circle far more regular than they can usually make with their eyes open.

Examples for working out various movement paths and linear shapes

During the lesson it so happens that a child has to come right across the room to the blackboard. This can be taken as a starting point. In which way can he travel? The quickest, of course, is the straight line but he can also arrive there on a curved or zigzag path. Where do we find such lines outside the teaching room (tram-lines, railway tracks, footpaths in a park, road junctions, patterns on fabrics and objects)?

—Who can draw such lines (in the air, on the floor with hands or feet, with chalk on the blackboard, with crayons or paint brushes on large sheets of

127

paper)? Before the children learn to walk along such paths in the room they should be able to draw them on a large or small scale, with each hand alone as well as with both hands together. Examples for possible movement paths are illustrated on p. 68.

With the help of obstacles certain paths can be mastered more easily.

—Stools are set out and the children walk alone or in a chain around these fixed points. Children can also take the place of the stools. (After a time there is a change-over.)

—One child leads a chain. At a call from teacher or child he leads the chain along different movement paths: from a circle into a serpentine pattern, from one corner right across the diagonal into the other corner, then in and out of a spiral or figure of eight and back again to the starting point.

—Once the children's space awareness is more strongly developed, this exercise can be practised with two chains. They can walk parallel to one another or they can trace the same figure, each using half of the room.

In doing so one group can walk or run forwards, the other backwards or sideways. The accompaniment to this can be played first in two-four and then in three-four time.

Examples for working in group formations and ways of holding

As soon as the children no longer move through space without relating to each other, a certain awareness of "in front of", "beside" or "behind" one another results quite naturally. At the same time one can join hands, or put hands and arms around shoulders or waists. Not all holds, however, are suitable for every movement. In the following examples various holds and group formations (see also pp. 69 – 71) are used.

—To a recorder melody the children move independently and freely round the room. When the tune stops they find a partner and dance with him when the melody starts up again. (Change from individual path to paths in pairs.)

—Instead of pairs, at an agreed signal the children form a group, a chain, a circle or a row.

—The children join hands in twos and skip round in a circle. Which holds are possible and which particularly suitable?

—The children run forwards in a chain with short, springy steps. Which way of holding is suitable when the steps are short, and which for long steps?

—They stand in a circle and move sideways using step and close, to the right and left. Different ways of holding are tried.

Mirror-image exercises

Observation and the exact rendering of a movement in space can be particularly well trained by mirror-image exercises. In so doing one starts from the experience that the mirror-image behaves and moves in exactly the same way (though with the sides reversed) as the person in front of the mirror. If this experience should be unfamiliar to any of the children they can easily catch up with the help of a mirror in the lesson.

128

—The children work together in pairs, between them is a "mirror". Everything done by one child must be imitated by the other, simultaneously but with the sides reversed. The exercises can conform to pantomimic or abstract concepts of movement.

Mirror-image exercises are not feasible in a group until the children have gained enough experience in working with a partner. All exercises can be done on the spot or in locomotion. It will, however, soon become obvious with the latter that movements with the back to the "mirror" for instance, are impossible for one's partner.

Introduction to various "forms"

These examples have a double purpose: The children should learn to recognise and realise elemental forms in music and movement and should achieve this through movement sequences that are also organised with reference to space, time and dynamics and that are combined with texts or melodies. Thus they will acquire the basic material which they will soon be able to utilise in recognisable forms.

The teacher should be given help and ideas in using her material and in making clear lesson plans. She and the children should have visible proof of the success of the lesson.

The elemental forms that concern us are as follows:

Repetition — echo

Completion — question and answer

Binary form — A-B

Three-part form — A-B-C; Ternary or song form — A-B-A or A-A-B-A

Rondo — A-B-A-C-A (to be extended through an optional number of episodes)

Canon — themes from the elements of rhythm, space or movement

Variation — repetition with modification

The children become familiar with these forms through "miniature" examples of only a few bars length. Visual links should be established as often as possible (photographs, drawings, sketches and examples that match the form concerned).

Repetition — echo

In repetition or echo exercises the child should comprehend a movement or rhythmic sequence and imitate it. With mirror-image work the reproduction is simultaneous, with echo work the one follows the other.

—The teacher plays a short melodic motif. The children listen and when the repetition starts they indicate this with a clap. They then try to find a movement that makes the repetition clearly recognisable.

—One child performs a short movement motif and the others try to repeat it. Did it turn out exactly the same or did one child make a slight change? When the original and the varied version are seen side by side, the difference can be seen

129

quite clearly. So, by chance a variation has been shown and has sharpened the faculty of observation.

—The children work in pairs on repetition and echo exercises of this kind. Each pair is working simultaneously but independently. The first child gives a rhythm and the other echoes it. The first moves according to the character and length of the rhythm (2, 4 or more bars) and the second tries to imitate exactly. After a while they change roles.

Completion – question and answer

Children know that in conversation questions and answers are exchanged. There are also games in which a child has to answer the questions of others. One can invent games of this kind in music and dance. The teacher (later a child) sings (claps, plays on a recorder or dances) a short phrase; the "answering" child continues and brings it to an end. Question and answer can (but do not have to) be of equal length. They can be similar, i.e. a certain rhythmic, melodic or dance motif can occur in both parts. They can also, however, present a sharp contrast to one another. It is important that question and answer, which only form a whole when they are together, should follow one another immediately. The structure of well-known songs should help to make this clear.

—We begin with a rhythmic exercise, in this case in the form of a question and answer. The teacher stands with the children in a circle. She claps a short phrase as question and the child next to her finds an answer. One after the other they answer the teacher's rhythmic questions, gradually extending their answers into movement and locomotion; steps that are stamped can become steps that travel forwards, backwards, sideways or ones that turn.

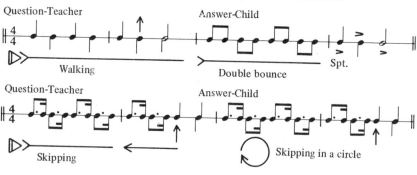

130

—Two rows stand facing one another. The children in the first row provide the question, and the others complete with the answer. One pair after another shows its own version, the others accompany with a quiet ostinato.

These exercises should not lack variety in time structure and phrase lengths, but should be developed as the experience of the children grows. The teacher can suggest that on one occasion two-four time, on another three-four or four-four time be used, and that the phrases be four or eight bars in length.

—As a variation small percussion instruments that can be played while moving (claves, finger cymbals, sleigh bells, castanets, coconut shells, tambours and tambourines, rattles and wood blocks) are added in performance. The movement must now match the instrument, i.e. instruments with a long reverberation produce quiet, sustained or swaying movements, those with a short, dry sound demand quick, agile ones.

—One child alone plays both question and answer and represents this in movement.

Binary form

Once the children have understood what the completion of a question through an answer means, then they have grasped the substance of all further forms. An A-B form arises when a longer statement, that is itself constructed as question and answer, is linked to a second statement containing contrasting subject matter, for example:

—The A part consists of a song. For the B part a short dance is added. Two circles are formed one inside the other. The inner circle dances the first part and the children accompany themselves on tambours. The outer circle takes over the B part to the accompaniment of a recorder.

—Are there other kinds of two-part form? Children find the most unusual answers: a church (tower and main body of church); maracas (head and handle); stool (seat with legs). Examples from music literature (also from records) provide new impressions for this theme.

Three-part – Ternary form

Various structures can be described as a three-part form. A-B-C, for instance, describes a form in which all three sections contain different subject matter. A-B-A or A-A-B-A contains only two sections whose subject matter differs, for these two forms arise from variously arranged repetitions. One finds these forms frequently in both songs and instrumental pieces. To these given forms one can evolve movement sequences that match the structure of the respective piece, but one can also start with the movement sequence and work out an accompaniment to it (purely rhythmic or rhythmic and melodic).

The children first experience the structure of a form in practical performance. By naming and describing the form they can then be made conscious of it. They practise recognising and naming such forms in pieces and songs that have already been used. Musical examples (possibly from different historical periods) should be used in this instance in order to extend individual experiences.

—The teacher plays or sings, claps or dances a phrase to which the children must pay close attention so that at the repetition they can join in. This will be made easier if they can discern the formal structure.

—The ostinati that have already been practised and that can be varied in so many ways are now used as building bricks for simple forms.

A-B-A form (in square formation)

A part: The rows marked 1, using the following ostinato, move towards one another (forte) and back to their original places (piano). The size of the square will determine how often the ostinato has to be played and this must be established in advance (e.g. two or four times).

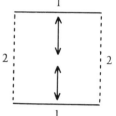

B part: In three-four time, performed with swinging walking steps. The two rows marked 2 turn so that their right shoulders point outwards and walk in chain formation behind the child who is leading at the time. This child leads across the diagonal to the opposite side, each chain therefore describing a big Z. To this the children add the finger snapping and patschen of the following rhythm (the snap is made with both hands alternately to the right and left).

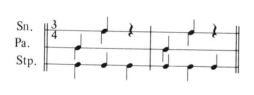

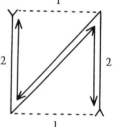

—Again the children look for examples of this form that have nothing to do with music or movement: window – door – window; cupboard – blackboard – cupboard. They can also build an A-B-A form with the objects to be found in the room; chair – table – chair; drum – recorder – drum.

Rondo

The name "rondo" can be traced back to a dance that was called "ronde" or "rondeau" which was probably danced round a tree on the village green. The first rondo will have a similar, simple, folk dance form.

—All children stand in a circle with the teacher. They sing and dance a short, well-known song during which they run or skip to the right and left. At the end of the song, the A part or the rondo theme, everyone stands and claps a simple

132

accompaniment to the teacher's recorder improvisation that has the same length as the song. Meanwhile a child can dance alone in the middle of the circle and he should find his way back to his place by the end of the middle section (the length will correspond to the words of the song that can be thought through silently).

Now everyone sings and dances the song once more followed by another child dancing the next episode, or he may choose for himself a partner to dance with. In this way we get a continuous alternation of song (tutti) and episode (solo) until every child has had a turn. A further performance of the song in which all are involved brings it to an end. Can one of the children describe what has just been made? Most of them have understood and try to describe it: "The part that always stays the same comes first, then something new is played and danced. The first part comes again and then something new and so on until the first part makes the ending.'

The usual model for a rondo is A-B-A-C-A. For rondo themes we can use dance songs, suitable texts, dance forms to instrumental music and also small rhythmic studies with instruments that are played while dancing. To make the episodes more varied the teacher should be clear about the different possibilities available for such tasks. The episodes must by no means always be improvised, one can use an already familiar melody, a movement combination or a text.

Suggestions for episodes
—Number of performers: If the rondo theme is performed by everyone (tutti) the episode, as a contrast, should be performed by an individual (solo), two or three children, or a small group.
—The use of space: Here, too, the episode should provide a contrast to the main theme. Where the main theme is performed in a circle, then the episodes can take the form of chains or rows.
—One child dances in the middle of the circle or threads his way in and out of the circle of children.
—One pair skips round in a small circle (holding right or left hands) and they should try to change the direction of their turning as often as possible.
—Another child remains in his place and improvises a simple stamped rhythm.
—Another might describe a figure of eight for his episode.
—An exercise in movement improvisation: To follow a quiet theme the first improviser should find a lively episode containing jumps.
—Another child should find as many different rhythmic step patterns as possible by alternating between the use of heels and balls of the feet.
—Three children hold hands and dance a sideways gallop interrupted by stamping.
—The teacher plays a recorder melody that is in a different time from that of the A part, thereby suggesting to the child that is improvising, for instance, a quiet, swinging movement in six-eight time.
—Including small percussion instruments and recorder: For one particular episode the soloist is given a tambourine to play while he dances.

—A child that plays the recorder particularly well accompanies his own movement, thereby learning to move so quietly that his breath is adequate for
moving and blowing.

—Two children improvise together. One holds claves and the other has sleigh
bells tied round his ankles. Their task is to find a question and answer in both
rhythm and movement.

As with three-part form rondo form can be represented in many ways, e.g.
buildings, decorative patterns and instruments.

Canon

Remind the children of a song that has already been sung in canon and consider if this form can be made clear in movement. Or begin with a miniature
example and talk about the form afterwards.

—A short movement sequence can be made by changing between travelling
skipping and quiet stamping on the spot.

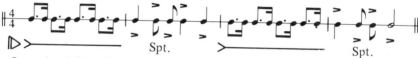

—Once the children have grasped the sequence and are able to do it the teacher
demonstrates with the help of one of them. She performs exactly the same
movement sequence as the child but starts a bar later. The watching children
are asked if they have noticed anything. Most of them will have understood
that the teacher simply started later but one might notice that the second entry
came just as the child was stamping on the spot.

—The same is now tried in two groups that stand in two rows facing one
another — 1 starts, 2 enters after one bar.

—Next they all stand in one row. Every second child belongs to the first group,
the others to the second. In this formation one can see the canon in movement
more clearly.

—Another time a song, that lends itself to canonic and dance treatment, is
worked out in music and movement. Here, too, the children can be stimulated
to think of a graphic representation of this form and to work at it together.
Further examples in working out rhythmic canons are to be found on pp.
191 and 202.

Variation

Variation form, both in music and in dance is rather advanced for work with
children. It is nevertheless quite possible to introduce variation form in small
examples worked out for oneself.

Rhythmic-movement theme

The teacher shows a short, very simple and clear movement sequence.

Walking forwards

The children watch the teacher's sequence and then repeat it. Finally each child varies the theme in his own way, though the basic sequence must remain recognisable.

Variation 1: Change step

C.S.   C.S.   C.S.   C.S.

Variation 2: Sideways cross-over step

out bef. out tog.   out bef. out tog.   out bef. out beh.   out bef. out tog.

Variation 3: Bouncing with change of direction

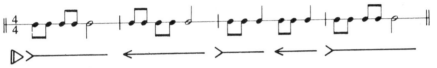

Variations on a spatial theme

The theme, that is to be varied by each child individually, is a circle that takes two bars of six-eight time and uses twelve steps.

Variation 1: The child walks backwards instead of forwards.

Variation 2: Instead of one large circle two small ones are made so that a figure of eight results.

Variation 3: A child walks so that his front is always facing forwards. To describe a circle without change of front he will now have to use cross-over steps as well as forwards and backwards.

The different verses of a song can be varied through the movement content as well as through movement paths and accompaniment.

Once the children understand the characteristics of the different forms, games that exercise aural and visual recognition can be introduced.

--A child thinks of a form and may show it by means of a rhythm, a melody, a drawing or a simple dance.

--Several children have worked out a form in movement. They show it to the others. Which form have they used? -- The others should know and recognise this as soon as possible.

When these elemental forms in music and dance have become familiar and natural to the children, and when they have experimented in making their own forms, then they are ready to carry this experience and knowledge into the field of Art.

Movement accompaniment

It is well-known from experience that music and movement have a strong reciprocal effect and that dancing can be influenced by its musical accompaniment, particularly in the spheres of choreographic form and the rhythmic, dynamic and expressive aspects of its performance.

What kind of an accompaniment is possible? When music and movement take place together they require equal artistic consideration and should correspond in style. It is a mistake to support simple, child-like movements with voluminous classical or romantic music. Movement should always adapt itself to music and music to movement. This reciprocal effect can be achieved when music is created for the situation of the moment, but not through the use of gramophone records. Should one use records of folk dance tunes, songs or instrumental pieces, they should be chosen with all the greater care.

It is advisable for the teacher to provide the accompaniment at first, but right from the start she should encourage the children to accompany the movement of their class-mates on various instruments, with speaking, singing and sound gestures. In this way music and movement may be adjusted to each other and correspond to the children's respective stage of development.

Every accompaniment can have, and especially at the beginning it must have, a structure that is clear and simple (short motifs with small variations are easier to understand than lengthy developments of motifs). It should be played dynamically, with plenty of variety and above all softly, so that the children learn to listen. Technical virtuosity on the teacher's part is unsuitable here but the accompaniment should be played imaginatively and in a lively manner. From time to time one may intentionally dispense with any accompaniment, thus preventing the children from relying solely on the externally given rhythm. Even without the accompaniment they should keep in time and maintain the feeling for phrasing. Apart from the requirements of the accompaniment there are also visual considerations. The teacher must be very much aware that her posture, when playing an instrument for example, will be copied by the children.

If one wants to accompany a movement sequence one must understand it, i.e. its tempo, dynamics, its time measure or metre, phrasing, character of movement, its accents and climaxes, must be experienced. This is best done by trying the movement out oneself. The ability to indicate the start of the accompaniment, to carry through a certain phrase and to finish it well, is developed through the exercises in time (see p. 113ff).

The accompaniment originates initially from the movement itself. The sound of steps forms the first acoustic background. The following examples show how one may build up the accompaniment starting from an acoustic or visual experience:

—The children sit in a circle facing the centre with their eyes closed. A child chosen beforehand, or the teacher herself now moves in various ways around the children (walking, running, skipping, tripping). The sound of the steps should not be exaggerated but should be just audible. The children should now listen to the steps with concentration and indicate the tempo with very soft clapping or patschen. The accompaniment should be quieter than the steps, for only then will it be possible to notice changes in tempo.

—All the children stand well spaced out round the hall; one child moves freely in the room and the others watch and try to accompany him. Should the movement change then the accompaniment must change accordingly.

The eyes are of course open during this exercise.

In the course of time more and more of the possible ways of accompanying are brought into action:

speaking and singing

sound gestures (clapping, patschen, finger-snapping and stamping)

small percussion instruments (tambour and tambourine, claves and castanets, rattles and maracas, sleigh bells, small cymbals, triangles, woodblocks and larger cymbals)

bongos

recorders

barred percussion (glockenspiels, xylophones, metallophones)

a small orchestra from all the listed instruments

a piano (as long as the teacher is able to improvise simply and in a suitable style)

The beginnings of movement accompaniment are now incorporated into the whole of the play activity.

—The children speak a text or sing a melody while dancing a round dance and a simple accompaniment can be added.

—Double circle: The children in the inner circle sing and move while the others stand in their places and accompany with clapping, stamping, etc. Then they change activities.

After some time the children try accompanying their movements with sound gestures or small percussion instruments. (In doing so the choice of instruments to be used must correspond to the character of the movement.)

—How can one accompany walking or running? Every child walks (runs) a few steps, then closes his eyes, imagines the tempo and finally plays the accompaniment on a tambour, on claves or simply claps. A more and more accurate idea of a tempo is established through the accompaniment. Even before the children have to indicate the start with an upbeat they must have a clear idea in their minds about the speed of their bouncing, jumping and walking.

—How is walking distinguished from skipping? Who can demonstrate the movement? Who can accompany it? (see p. 76ff)

—Three groups stand in the room. Followed by the rest of his group the leader of the first starts with a movement; he describes a large circle ending in his original place; the second group accompanies, every child inventing his own clap-stamp rhythm. After this the second group moves while the third takes over the accompaniment. Each group should, as far as possible, choose its own type of movement.

—Some children run around alone (or in pairs or small groups) while the others try to accompany the tempo of one predetermined child with claves: at a signal from the teacher the claves are exchanged, those who played the accompaniment now run.

—Children holding sleigh bells form a row along the diagonal. The distances between the individual children are large enough to allow the rest of the children to skip one at a time around those who are standing. While they now skip, gallop, jump or run, the children who are standing accompany their movements. After a while they change activities. This time, started by one child who sets the tempo, the accompaniment gives the lead and the movement adapts itself to it.

—One child stands with a triangle, another with finger cymbals; they play alternately but without a set rhythm. Half the children listen to the cymbals, the others to the triangle. With each beat the corresponding group moves on the spot for as long as the sound can be heard.

The following exercise trains the ability to follow various changes of tempo in the accompaniment:

—The children sit in a large circle while the teacher moves with gradual or sudden changes of tempo. They watch with great concentration and accompany — sometimes with one child playing on his own, sometimes all together.

The inclusion of barred percussion instruments and recorders adds a further dimension to movement accompaniment. Once the very first instrumental difficulties have been overcome the children will be able to play simple ostinati on xylophones together with short improvised melodies on glockenspiels or recorders; the melody could also be sung. Question and answer produce a certain phrasing which again brings about a clear structure in the movement. By this time the rhythmic structure of the accompaniment can be varied freely since it need no longer be tied to the basic rhythm of the movement.

As soon as confidence in forming melodies and playing simple accompaniments has been achieved, several instruments may be put together to form a small orchestra. Some barred percussion instruments can have various complementary ostinati with two or three melody parts taking it in turns. Other percussion instruments are added sparingly as tone colour and to provide rhythmic support for the movement.

The teacher must of course give guidance in the build-up of such an accompaniment. After some practice the children themselves will offer ideas that are examined by teacher and class together, improved by further suggestions and thus developed into a suitable form.

Besides these original and partly improvised accompaniments, instrumental pieces or songs can also be played as accompaniments to movement. No limits are set for musical ideas. The degree of difficulty of the accompaniment will correspond to the general level of the children's ability. The further one can develop musical feeling, technical ability, theoretical knowledge and understanding of form, the richer and more varied the accompaniment will become.

138

Guidelines for the development of such accompaniments and for the use of instrumental pieces are to be found mainly in the sample lessons. (p. 175) Movement can be accompanied rhythmically, melodically, harmonically or with speech, though it by no means always has to be. In the absence of any accompaniment silence adds intensity to accent and transition, to the individually chosen tempo. Here it is also essential that movement is not metrically fixed, but that its rhythm corresponds to the character of the movement used by the child at that moment; such movement is more subjective and individual by nature than movement that is subjected to an accompaniment. Accompaniment should particularly be dispensed with at the beginning of experiments with new tasks where the child first has to adapt himself to his own reactions – these in turn being dependent on his individual speed of movement.

Themes for composition in this field can be drawn from any sphere; tasks can be set in the realms of space, time or dynamics, and can be worked out singly, in pairs, in small or larger groups. Themes arising specifically from movement or from the body are specially suitable. Parts of the body, for example, can be moved simultaneously, in sequence, in symmetrical, parallel or asymmetrical directions; the flow of movement can be interrupted or sustained, be in a straight line or a curve, be direct or indirect, according to the spatial factor in view. Possibilities for simple composition can be stimulated during partner work: repeating something similar or answering in a strong contrast.

Unaccompanied movement differs basically from accompanied movement in that it possesses a stronger concentration on the personal inner rhythm, while movement that is accompanied has to adjust to an external rhythm. In teaching it is advisable to take both types into consideration.

Improvisation

This should be included in every lesson, not indeed as an isolated task but as an educational principle that is part of a creative way of working. This makes special demands on the teacher. She has to consider carefully which part of the prepared material is suitable for improvisation, and how the children's ability to improvise can be systematically improved. A great deal, and much of it controversial, has been written about the concept of "improvisation". In this book we understand by improvisation the child's spontaneous handling of completely or partially known material.

Improvisation can lead to a clearly distinguishable form, but it can also be playing with new ideas that are not in any way fixed. It can certainly be considered as promoting creative attitudes.

Tasks for improvisation can be set at the beginning or at the end of a period of working with new material. In the first case every child experiments with the theme in his own way, and from all the various solutions several of general and fundamental validity are chosen and practised by all participants.

--As an accompaniment the teacher plays a dotted rhythm, and the children try to match their movement to it. One will see hopping on one leg, skipping and gallop jumps. Some children will skip in a straight line -- others will turn around. There will be different ways of holding the arms and of moving the working leg. After some solutions have been shown the other children try to imitate them.

Here improvisation is a starting point leading to imitation. The following example shows the process in reverse.

--Skipping forwards and backwards, sideways and turning, also high and wide skips combined with different kinds of intermediate steps, and then a variety of rhythms and dynamics are practised. Now the children are asked to try out a longer movement sequence or simple dance on the theme 'skipping' with this raw material. A melody or an already familiar piece of music is given, or the movement sequence is not accompanied at all. Each child may try out his own movement paths and patterns, sequence of steps and dynamic shape. This exercise can be carried out alone, in twos or threes, but also in small groups. The individual solutions are demonstrated, the other children or the teacher possibly adding relevant suggestions. Finally a definite form is evolved that can be repeated and noted down.

Improvisation can lead to composition in two ways that can be combined:
Experimental improvisation, followed by practice at basic forms, leads to the creation of small forms.
Basic forms are worked out and create the preconditions for a spontaneous adaptation into small, individual dance forms.

We can distinguish:

Individual improvisation (This is not synonymous with 'solo' improvisation but means that many children improvise simultaneously and independently.)

Improvisation with partners (in twos, threes or fours)

Improvisation in groups (larger or smaller groups)

Fundamentally the whole of the material discussed in this book can also be given to the children in the form of exercises in improvisation. When formulating exercises for improvisation it must be borne in mind that children ought not to be given total freedom in the sense of the notorious 'Do whatever comes into your head'. From experience we know that they feel especially insecure in that situation and perhaps not all their ideas will be realisable at the moment – for example 'shadow games'.

The theme for the exercise in improvisation should be discussed and clarified with the children beforehand; sufficient scope for individual solutions should, however, be allowed. Two examples should make this clear.

Individual improvisation

During a general discussion on the theme "fairground", planned to cover several sessions, one child tells of a dancer who danced on a tiny stage. There is unanimous agreement that this should be included in the programme.

Characteristic features which are later given as stimulation for improvisation must be discovered: spatial limitations due to the stage (movements needing wide spaces are, therefore eliminated; bouncing movements with varied positions for the working leg, turns on the spot or small steps with frequent changes of direction seem to be more suitable). Should the girl – it can of course also be a boy – dance with or without music? The girl whose idea this dance was, suggested that a tambourine played by the soloist should be the only accompaniment.

From this collection of ideas the following exercises can be developed:

–In a limited space (where no small stage blocks are available the space can be marked by a rope laid on the floor) movements should be tried out and in fact limited to bouncing movements with varied position of the working leg, turns and small side and close steps with change of direction.

–How can this material be formed into a small, three-part dance? How can a contrast be achieved in the middle part? (It would be possible through using steps that had not been tried previously, or through a noticeable change of tempo.)

–Finally the accompaniment must be incorporated. How can the tambourine be held? Are the steps too complicated to be combined with the tambourine accompaniment? What simple accents in the movement can be found?

Despite the fact that the task is more precisely characterised through spatial factors and the choice of the accompanying instrument, each child has sufficient freedom to find an individual solution unlike any other.

Improvisation in small groups on the theme: playing small percussion instruments while dancing.

Handling sleigh-bells, claves and tambour is familiar to the children. Each child chooses one of the three kinds of instrument according to what is available.
—How can one play the instrument and move at the same time? How will the type of movement affect the way the instrument is held? The greatest number of possibilities should be found.
—Small groups (each comprising three or four children) are formed. Each group agrees on a motif for locomotion. How does the accompaniment sound? It need not be in unison but should fit together well. (The children with sleigh-bells on their ankles will have chosen stamping rhythms, those with claves should make use of the space around them and also of the floor. The children with tambours may perhaps find a solution in which they alternately play their own drums and that of their partner.)
—Each group chooses a place in the room. One after the other they show their solutions while the others accompany very quietly or just watch. The movement path of each group is determined by a leader. When the first group has returned to its starting place, then the next one begins.

Finally: What differences could one see, for example, in the type of movement, the movement paths, group formations and accompaniment?

Composition of dances

Many examples will show how dance compositions originate on the one hand from the children's improvisation and on the other hand from the purposeful linking together of practice exercises. They can also be worked out by teachers and children together during the lesson, or they can be prepared as homework. The starting points for a dance composition are varied.

Movement

—The children are asked to develop a small movement form to the theme 'running-dance'. Running in a circle or in a chain, in twos or alone, in various floor patterns or directions — this is the basic material.

—From exercises with partners and with balls a simple sequence arises that should show possibilities of playing with a ball (rolling, throwing, passing, bouncing). Here the structure develops from play and improvisation.

—As an exercise each child should think of a short phrase of movement using claves. The most suitable solution can be used as an episode in a rondo. To help and give stimulation the teacher should discuss various possibilities beforehand: different ways of playing and holding the instrument, the inclusion of the floor as a striking surface, combination with particular types of movement and dance steps.

Imaginative or mimed scenes

—This comprises the spontaneous creation of individual roles from fairy tales, action songs or texts. For example, in Tweedledum and Tweedledee (p. 185) the characters of the two heroes can be differently portrayed by each child. Characteristic details are discussed with the children beforehand: how the monstrous crow will move; how the heroes will show their fear. Other possibilities can be found in the sample lessons (pp. 181, 194 and 207).

Music

—The teacher plays a piece of music that is already familiar to the children, something from Orff-Schulwerk or from Bartók's Mikrokosmos, for example. If one of the children is competent in playing an instrument (the recorder, piano or other instrument) he should be encouraged to do so. The other children form various small groups and try to create a dance to the music. Such teamwork is unlikely to succeed at the first attempt since it needs preparation through many simple exercises.

143

—Basic musical forms such as binary and ternary form, rondo and canon that occur in songs and instrumental pieces that are worked at in the music lessons are then interpreted in dance. Portable instruments (barred percussion, drums, recorders, etc.) can be brought into the dance room. For details see the sample lessons pp. 178 and 202.

Whether the initial impulse for a dance composition comes from a movement, an imagined scene or from music, creative possibilities for composing dances are found in the following:

Dance songs, singing games, action songs

Dance songs are those whose texts express a particular association with dancing and music. The content of the movement is not the important consideration. The material consists of patterns of steps and movement combinations with as many spatial variations as possible. Singing games and action songs have dramatic themes that can be stylised or mimed.

Texts (rhymes, riddles, proverbs, fairy-tales)

The individual texts supply different ideas for composition. Counting rhymes are self-explanatory. Riddles are only of use when the object to be guessed can be represented. Magical sayings inspire the children to new movements that correspond to the mysterious text. Saying fables and texts from fairy tales give stimulation for mimetic work. (see pp. 175, 176, 181, 183, 185 and 187)

Dances to instrumental pieces

Simple pieces that the children can play themselves can be chosen. From time to time a gramophone record or recorded tape can be used in order to show richer instrumentation or a musically inspiring interpretation. (see p. 194)

Rhythmical studies with or without instruments

The types of movement that are accompanied by sound gestures or by small percussion instruments that are played while dancing belong to this category. As a variation an accompaniment can be chosen that is played, perhaps on bongos, bass drum or gong, by a child who is not dancing. The rhythms and corresponding movements can be in the form of ostinati or in continuous phrases, monophonic or polyphonic. All the exercises that were discussed in the chapter 'Introduction to various forms' can be used. (see also pp. 191 and 202)

Part Four
Survey of Material According to Age Groups

General aspects of the arrangement of material

Guidance in the arrangement of subject matter is requested again and again by students and teachers. The general validity of such guidance is made more difficult, however, by the different teaching conditions (classes being given both inside and outside the school situation, classes of different sizes, differences in aptitude, insufficient basic training).

Suggestions for selection and organisation of material given here should be taken as a framework only. Nursery School teachers, Primary School teachers, teachers of music, gymnastics and dance must adapt it to their individual teaching situation.

—The subject matter presented here is designed to start in the nursery school and be continuously developed through to the fourth or fifth year of schooling (9 – 10 years old). The suggested plan can only be successfully realised if a start is made with children at the age of about four years. Where this is not possible, adjustment in the selection of material would have to be made — for example the material suggested for "advanced" six-year-olds would be more suited to a beginner of eight years of age.

—Choice of material is always dependent on the psychological and physical development of the children, their aptitude and capacity, their imagination and concentration as well as on the influence of the home environment. These factors differ in each group of children. Therefore the guidelines set forth here should be extended or shortened by the teacher according to the circumstances of her class. Sometimes it will be necessary to go back to the exercises for younger children — at other times the examples for older children may already have to be used.

—Frequently the various age groups are given the same or similar exercises; this is entirely realistic. With slight adaptations they usefully repeat and reinforce previous experiences.

—Progress is dependent on the size of the group. Carefully thought out correction, guidance in creative work, observation of all individual solutions must be inadequate with groups of forty children. In these cases it is necessary to divide the class (accepted procedure in other subjects) in the interest of the children and of worthwhile progress.

—Improvisation is not an independent field but an integrated part of teaching. From each of the undermentioned sections tasks may be set in such a way that they can be solved by the children through improvisation.

—Exercises for training the senses, for concentration, co-ordination and skill, for adaptation, organisation, leadership and responsibility, for the development of awareness of space and form and sensitivity towards working in groups, are not given separately. Since almost every task has several educational aims it is left to the teacher to emphasise those factors that correspond to the situation relevant to an individual child or to the whole group.

—Reaction exercises not only serve to train attentiveness, the power to make decisions and the quick transformation of decision into activity. They also enable the teacher to recognise the extent to which the children are capable of relating their ability in movement with external challenges and signals. Reaction exercises, however, should in no circumstances be used merely for the purpose of discipline. They must be combined with tasks which demand much creative work.

—The reaction can be a response to aural, visual, verbal and, in rare cases, also to tactile stimuli. The items listed in the tabulated summary should be used for a variety of tasks.

—In the first part of the book detailed material can be found that is relevant to the subject in the tabulated survey named "Movement training" (movement experiment, body training, basic types of movement and movement combinations). For 'Group formations and ways of holding' see the drawings on pp. 69 – 73.

—Movement accompaniment is largely determined by the group's music lessons and may possibly be discussed and arranged with the music teacher.

—Examples of "Movement compositions" are to be found in Part Five.

Characteristics of the three age ranges

Age range 1: Four to six years

During the nursery school years the fundamentals for any later training are laid. At this age dance education does not represent an individual subject. On the contrary, combined with music and language development it is integrated into the daily programme of the nursery school. One long or two short periods should be used for this daily. The content of the lesson will have to be chosen according to whether the work takes place in a room suitable for movement, in the music room or in a classroom.

The starting point is free individual or group movement play. In free movement play (rocking, balancing, turning, tripping along, 'dancing on tiptoes', rolling, crawling) in all the numerous and repeated variations, the child experiments with his particular physical possibilities. He trains his skill and co-ordination, his feeling for the dimensions of space and for various speeds; he learns to know the individual parts of his body and the functions of his movements; he tests the working out of his own movement impulses.

In group movement play, but above all in traditional children's games and dances which are tied to rhythm and speech, he experiences the necessity to adapt to others and to function as one of a group. The movement is determined by a common tempo and by certain rules externally imposed upon the individual child. To compensate for this co-operation and subordination most children vie for those occasions when they can work freely and as a soloist.

With this age group it is vitally important to maintain the children's original pleasure in and spontaneous need for movement, and to be continuously setting new tasks which will interest them in a wide range of movement experiences and to stimulate them to experiment. There is a gradual transition to specific movement sequences, forms and reactions. It is not imitation of the teacher that is important but the unhindered, imaginative and flowing movement of each individual child. Technical perfection is a later aim, though even at this age the child should be made aware of his posture.

Since children's concentration cannot at this age be held for long on one theme it is advisable to change the main points of interest frequently, thereby giving relief from movement through singing, instrumental playing, speech or through experiments with pre-notation. Constant repetition of fixed sequences overtaxes their powers of concentration and tires them.

Age range 2: Six to eight years

The lessons now take place within the framework of the primary school and are usually given by the class teacher rather than a specialist. Despite some difficulties this has the advantage that it can bring about better integration of the various fields of teaching. Because of her thorough knowledge of her class the teacher can give exercises and tasks that have either general educational aims, or aims that are specifically concerned with music or dance education.

Opportunities for work out of school are to be found in junior classes of a music school (college of music, music schools run by the state or privately), in dancing or gymnastic schools or in leisure activity groups. If good results are to be achieved, the principle that lessons should occur as often as possible — preferably daily at school — is still valid.

The child has developed psychologically and physically; these changes must be considered when teaching. Increased growth in height and development of the inner organs affects the kinds of physical demands that can be made. Periods of movement should be short and intensive; effort must be followed by periods of rest which can, however, be filled with rhythmical exercises, singing, speech or instrumental work, aural exercises and notation practice.

This is still a time for descriptive plays, of identification with various roles and characters. To this, however, is added the aspiration to learn and to be able to achieve; the first sign of objective thinking is seen. Beside children's group dances and plays on the one hand and individual experiments in movement on the other, various basic types of movement are worked out. This occurs in variations relating to space, time and dynamics, based on the experience gained in the previous stage. The adaptation to other children is also slowly developed (in group formations, exercises in leading and partner work). The effect of developing powers of observation is shown through the awakening interest in the 'what, how and where' of a movement, in the recognition of mistakes and in the pleasure of imitation. Nevertheless the individual solution of movement tasks must not be neglected.

Musical ability and knowledge have also been extended; through the encounter with books the world of a child's imagination has been enlarged. All this ought to be borne in mind in relation to dance education.

Since the children have to sit a great deal at school and when doing their homework the accumulated motor need unloads itself in playing and in the movement lessons. Allowance must be made for this, but concentration and discipline during the lesson should not suffer because of it.

Age range 3: Eight to ten years

If the music and movement teaching is still being given by the class teacher then, if at all possible, lessons should occur daily for a short period, or at least three times weekly. Should these subjects be taught by a specialist (music, or dance teacher or physical education specialist) then close collaboration and a common teaching plan is strongly advised. In this case some items will be prepared in the music lessons and others during the physical education or dancing lessons. In a combined lesson the connection between movement and music will be established. If need be the class teacher can repeat the movement forms, songs and accompaniments during her lessons. In extra-curricular groups the progress in this age range will be more noticeable than that in the school classes. This is mainly because of the more intensive general guidance and correction which a smaller group makes possible.

In this age group the second stage of rapid physical growth is concluded; the motor impulse has changed. Through the physical development and the resulting bodily adjustment comes an excess of energy that wants to express itself in movement and effort. Increased co-ordination, confidence and differentiation in the performance of a movement makes quicker comprehension of new movement relationships possible. This is supported by greater powers of observation, by a growing understanding for relationships in form and by the increasing ability to store the experience of movement in the memory. The will to achieve and interests directed towards a specific aim begin to change the child's attitude. He no longer wants 'only to play' — he wants to learn and to achieve — he wants to compare his own achievement with that of others. Group sensitivity, adaptation and responsibility are increasing.

At this age the type of movement and the interests of boys and girls begin to differ. Common to both is a greater concern with objective skills and a desire to be told what to do. For this reason one can now introduce the children to traditional dance forms, but should also draw their attention to related forms that lie outside their ability. Their understanding of different styles of dancing ought to be awakened by photos, films, possibly theatre visits, general discussion of dance productions on television (folk dances of other countries, jazz, shows, modern dance or ballet, social dancing).

The material for boys has to be chosen and presented especially carefully so that the opinion that dancing is a feminine concern is not formed. It is up to the teacher to refute this prejudice through her teaching, her own example, but also through explanations, photographs and examples. The tasks for boys should require more strength and skill than those for girls. Steps from dances for men — from their own country as well as from other countries — can be included in the lessons.

Since examples are always more convincing than explanations it would be highly desirable if from time to time the class were taken by a man.

The material for girls is also extended by folk dances. Swinging movements can be started at the appropriate stage of physical maturity. Tasks for improvisation and invention should be set for all the children together. These should stimulate the imagination which is investigating new spheres of movement, technical achievement, physical energy and psychological awareness.

The material for this age range is built up on the basic material already used in earlier stages. It is extended and differentiated. The mastering of different dances and dance forms is added to the extension of the individual experience of movement and technique.

Tabulated Survey of Classified Material

	Age range 1
Movement training	Work starts with and emphasises play, both free and imitative; it includes equipment, partners and mimetic scenes. Exercises as an end in themselves are not suitable for this age group.
Movement experiment	Stimulated by free play, the functional possibilities of the individual parts of the body (head, trunk, arms, hands, legs, feet) are experienced through touching, moving and naming them; the setting of tasks using equipment (scarves, canes, small bean bags, ropes, smaller and larger balls) and the imitation of people, animals or objects.
Body training	
Relaxation and loosening-up exercises	General relaxation exercises after strenuous activity: lying on the back to calm down breathing; active shaking of legs and arms; passive relaxation exercises are only to be used for children who are especially tense, and here the teacher always takes over the active, helping role. (Imaginative stimuli may be useful.)

Age range 2	Age range 3
The children begin to understand the functions of movement and the variability of the basic types of movement; adaptation to a partner, spatial factor and equipment; transition from imaginative tasks to abstract ones.	Differentiated movement performance with variations related to space and time; increasing familiarity with movement terminology; setting of tasks that are predominantly abstract nevertheless does not exclude imaginative ones.
The various movement possibilities of the individual parts of the body are experienced. What: head, neck, shoulders, pelvis, leg, knee, foot, arm, elbow, hand, finger. Where: forwards – backwards, high – low, side – side, far – near. How: quickly – slowly, simultaneously – successively, lightly – with tension.	As for age range 2 with additional refinement of observation and performance. What: the whole body or parts, which part of the body is leading, to which side. Where: straight or curved lines, in the air and on the floor. How: symmetrical, flowing, interrupted, uniform or changing in tension and tempo. Movement experiments above are also possible as tasks with partners, as are mirror image or movement in contrast.
As for age range 1; the passive relaxation exercises, if necessary, with the help of the teacher.	As for age range 2; when setting exercises for relaxation, the increasing tension, brought about by sitting still at school and while doing homework, has to be taken more into consideration.

153

Tension exercises

At this stage the tension exercises only serve the purpose of letting the child experience his own total bodily energy.

Exercises for posture

First drawing of attention to an upright, relaxed posture without a hollow back and without turning the toes inwards; learning to recognise straight or round-shouldered sitting or standing (p. 58).

In connection with training for posture, exercises for balancing may also be tried, such as balancing on a line drawn on the floor or on a rope (child possibly supported by teacher), later also on equipment, such as long forms, small boxes and stools.

Strengthening exercises

Extreme bending, straightening and twisting of the whole body or of individual parts (arms and legs, trunk) while standing, sitting and lying down, at first slowly, then more quickly. Strengthening of the feet through spreading out and contracting, gripping exercises with the toes with the help of small objects (p.60). Strengthening the trunk through exercises done while lying on stomach or back; alternate or simultaneous lifting of legs and arms, using small objects held in the hand especially small bean bags (p. 61).

Age range 2	Age range 3

As for age range 1; add tension exercises of the whole body in play form as well as partial tension exercises – in each case the period of tension should only be of very short duration.

As for age range 2; add quicker change between partial tension and relaxation exercises (pages 52 and 55).

Bringing into consciousness for the first time the physical make-up relating to posture, namely, all joints one above the other: knee above ankle, hips above knees, shoulder girdle above pelvic girdle, straightening of spine while keeping pelvis in an upright position. (p. 58 – 60) Balancing exercises as for age range 1, also while walking on the ball of the foot, possibly with eyes closed.

Making aware of physical make-up of posture in both standing and sitting; learning to observe one's own posture as well as that of one's class-mates, on the spot and in locomotion (p. 58 – 60). Balancing exercises are made more difficult by changing focus of eyes as well as by simultaneous gestures of arms, legs or trunk, both on the spot and in locomotion.

Bending, straightening and twisting the whole body as for age range 1. Increase the speed during the exercise. Strengthening the foot through bending, straightening, rotating, gripping exercises, exercises in bouncing using the ankle.
Strengthening the trunk as for age range 1; using medium sized or larger balls as well as canes, also exercises with partners (pp. 60 – 61).

As for age range 2; add strengthening the foot through bending and straightening exercises with and without weight-bearing; touching the floor with different parts of the foot (toes, ball, heel, inner and outer edges) in free or metric rhythm; bouncing while squatting, standing and in locomotion, with feet together, alternately from right to left, or repeated bounces on one leg. Strengthening of the trunk through intensive activity of the stomach and back muscles while lying, sitting and standing (careful control of posture), with and without gymnastic equipment.

155

Basic types of movement

Walking

On the whole foot, high on the ball of the foot, with straight knees or with bent knees lifted high; forwards, later also backwards (not yet with accompaniment); along straight paths (from one side of the room to the other, or diagonal), along curved paths around obstacles (other children, stools, etc.). Increase from slow to fast (use train as imaginative stimulus); only in duple or quadruple time. From very light up to forceful. Alone, in a crowd, in twos. The accompaniment can help to keep a steady beat; nevertheless constant giving of tempo by the teacher prevents child from choosing a spontaneous one; very quiet accompaniment can educate the children to walk quietly (walking on the ball of the foot, rolling action of the foot).

Running

With short or long steps; adapting to the space and to the other children; along straight or curved paths; with, later also without, solid obstacles; forwards only.
From medium to very fast tempo (tripping). Light and quiet running.
Alone, in twos (first without, later with holding).
Adaptation to accompaniment, also free running without a fixed rhythm.

As for age range 1; add long or short steps, emphasis on high and low level.

Change of direction forwards and backwards, right and left (at first in a slow speed and with rests (musical) later with a smooth transition); walking sideways with side and close and cross-over steps. At about seven years introduction of walking in three-four time, in simple rhythmic patterns (doubling or halving speed of step).

Indicate accented beat with a stamp or with low level emphasis. In twos or threes, holding with one or both hands.

Characterise the walking in dramatic play (King, Red Indians, etc.).

As for age range 2; in all directions (forwards, backwards, sideways); add turning while walking; in zigzag, in large and small curves; with changes of direction and front.

Swinging walk (mainly for girls); low, medium and high level walking with frequent changes; walking in various floor patterns (circle, figure of eight, etc.) also with eyes closed.

In gradual and sudden changes of tempo.

Various rhythms.

In twos and threes, in a chain and in a row; holding with crossed hands.

Various forms of expression (sauntering, striding, strutting, prowling, hesitant) set in a mimetic task.

Striding out with long steps and running with small steps (tripping); arms hanging free or hands on hips; forwards and backwards; running around obstacles as preparation for running in a curve; changes in direction. At about seven years begin running in three-four time (stress on accented first beat); medium to fast tempo; easy and tensed running (exercise for the preparatory run for a jump).

Holding in twos (starting with parallel feet, i.e. both r. or both l.) in chains.

With and without accompaniment; running in three-four time is supported by a melodic accompaniment and a clearly given accent.

Forwards and backwards; also with turning while running; changes of front and direction; running in curves leaning towards the centre the arms carried stretched out sideways, in figures of eight. Working out of different types of running (emphasis high and bouncing, swinging, leaping).

In barrings (measures) with both an even and an uneven number of beats, gradual transitions of tempo from medium to fast.

Various ways of holding that can also be changed while running, in twos and threes, chains and rows. With and without accompaniment.

Bouncing

On the spot only (squatting or in upright position) with feet together (see body training). (p. 61)

Skipping

Skipping forwards; accompaniments (it is best to use six-eight time) should not always be used; some children need a relatively long time to learn to skip. Medium tempo.
Alone, in a crowd, later in twos; holding hands only when skipping is secure.

Bouncing on the spot with feet together up to point where toes start to lose contact with the floor; first attempts at alternate bouncing by jumping from one leg to the other forwards only; possibly double bouncing.
Medium tempo.
So far without holding.

Single, double and multiple bouncing on one leg, on the spot and in locomotion; forwards, backwards, sideways (cross-over and step and close), turning; always with emphasis on upward lift.
Free leg with knee bent or straight, ankle straight or bent; lifting the working leg forwards, backwards or sideways. Tempo in regular beats; later also in different rhythms freely changing between single and double bouncing.
With light or with very powerful pressure away from the floor.
All known ways of holding, but not before bouncing is secure.

Still only simple "children's skipping" with the free leg lifted up and bent; forwards, long and short steps; emphasis on upward lift.
Medium tempo, triplets, later dotted rhythms.
Light to energetic.
Alone, in a crowd, in twos, chains, rows; ways of holding as loose as possible.

With varied positions of the free leg (straight or bent in ankle and knee joints, lifted up forwards, sideways or backwards, or crossed over in front of or behind the supporting leg).
In all directions; sideways with step and close or cross-over steps, while turning; all known floor patterns and group formations; in combination with intermediate steps. Long and short skips, skipping high or normally.
Medium to fast, dotted rhythms and triplets, with an even and with an uneven number of beats in a bar; light and swinging to very strong. Holding in twos, in threes, in a chain and a row; when holding, the more distant from one another the more intensive the movement can be.

Jumping

Free jumping over small obstacles; jumping off low equipment (benches, stools) to practise take-off and landing; they should try to land quietly; preparatory run for jump of child's own choice as climax; run after landing to be practised freely.

"Gallop jump" forwards, jumping off alternate legs; at about five years the difference between skipping and gallop jump should be made clear. Jumping from one to two feet in walking, possibly going down to a squatting position at the end of a sequence (about five years).

At first without, later with accompaniment (paying attention to preparatory run and follow-through run).

Swaying with transfer of weight

Turning

Freely on the spot (imaginative stimuli — spinning top, toy windmill).

160

Free jumps from running or standing; various ways of taking off and landing should be tried individually.

"Gallop jump" with emphasis both upwards and in direction of travel; forwards, soon also turning.

The jump from one to two feet while walking and running, first simply, then with a half turn.

At about seven years, introduction of the scissors jump.

General jumping qualities to be developed; powerful take-off, good posture in the air, quiet, soft landing on the floor.

Swaying movement on the spot including the use of equipment (small bean bags and balls), later also transfer of weight forwards-backwards (one foot in front of the other) and right-left (feet apart).

Free or within a given task (maintaining direction, changing direction, certain number of steps) still mainly on the spot.

On whole foot or on ball of the foot; with slow step and close or quick tripping steps.

In combination with locomotion (walking, running, skipping).

Free jumps from standing as well as from all known ways of locomotion; examples of each of the five ways of jumping should be tried out; landing also in the squatting position.

Gallop jump forwards and turning. The jump from one to two feet forwards and sideways (possibly also backwards), from walking, running bouncing and skipping with half and whole turns.

Heel-click jumps to the side can be attempted.

Scissors jump forwards with a turn (with partner ready to give assistance).

Sitting jumps and small splits jumps on the spot.

Leaping and running and leaping.

Developing from the swinging of a piece of equipment and swaying the body forwards-backwards, right-left, to the swinging walk and run; at about nine years turns can be tried, mainly for girls.

As for age range 2; add support of rotation through position of arms (opening and closing) and head (fixing eyes on one point and at last minute a quick turn of the head to fix the eyes on the same point again). Turning in a low, medium and high position (correspondingly on the whole foot with bent knees, standing up with straight knees and standing tall on the ball of the foot); turning through all three levels (spirals) possibly with the help of equipment (doubly coiled rope). Turning on one leg (bouncing), on two legs with feet together (small jumps turning). In combination with all known means of locomotion.

161

Sound gestures	Clapping, patschen, possibly also stamping; at first each on his own, later in the simplest combinations.
	Combining stamping and clapping (a difficult co-ordination exercise for children) first at a slow tempo on the spot.
	Combining clapping and walking.
	Simple, short rhythms, also as accompaniment to texts or songs.

Movement combinations

Simultaneous performance of two or more types of movement	In free play with equipment (light scarves, balloons, balls are especially suitable) the play-idea results in locomotion in combination with bending, stretching, turning; trunk and arms adapt themselves to the equipment. Walking (possibly running) with clapping; at first without specific phrasing, only travelling forwards; later clapping in time with the steps, then twice as fast and twice as slow, or accompany with short rhythmic motifs; instead of clapping, claves or small tambours can be played; also to be used for echo exercises done in chain formation.
	Combination of types of locomotion close to the floor: crawling, rolling, sliding, creeping.
	Similarly in an upright position; walking and running with turns.
	A precise change of movement is not yet possible.
Two or more types of movement carried out in succession	Changing between walking, running, skipping, gallop jumps; at first without distinct phrasing, as a reaction exercise to the specific accompanying rhythm, later in distinct phrases; precise transitions are not yet possible.

As for age range 1; add stamping and finger-snapping (some children have difficulties with this at first); simple combinations.

Smooth co-ordination of two or three possibilities, with both an even and an uneven number of beats in the bar, on the spot and in locomotion.

As for age range 2; combining all four possibilities on the spot and in locomotion, in all known kinds of time and time changes, in combination with all basic types of movement.

As for age range 1; non-metrical movement playing freely with equipment; also with partners or in a group. Walking, running, skipping in combination with sound gestures; with an even number of beats, later with an uneven number in the bar, to accompanying rhythms that are fixed or improvised; similarly the playing of small percussion instruments to movement.

Combining various means of locomotion with turns and jumps (also including locomotion close to the floor).

Experimenting and practising with equipment (balls, ropes, hoops) in combination with movement on the spot and in locomotion.

Alone, with partner or group.

Inclusion of sound gestures in more difficult combinations to all known means of locomotion, also with turning or bending the trunk; the use of claves, finger cymbals, tambours and tambourines, sleigh bells and cymbals.

Swinging, walking and running (mostly for girls); running and leaping, turning jumps and the free combination of all known ways of moving.

As for age range 1; but different phrasings should be worked out, e.g. the change from eight to eight, four to four bars for each type of movement; from time to time take into consideration regularly recurring phrases with

Combination of all known types of locomotion in shorter and shorter phrases; also with change of direction; with doubling or halving the basic tempo; e.g. six walking steps forwards (crotchets), then double bounces in a

Reaction training

Space

From free running (walking, skipping) coming to a stop at a certain acoustic signal and finding one's bearings in the room: Where is in front, where are the windows, where is the teacher?
Gathering in certain corners, in the middle or on one side of the room, evenly spaced in the whole hall; forming a circle, later also a row (at first with the help of one of the walls) then pairs. A certain part of the body (hand, knee, tip of the nose) should move in a forward, upward, downward direction; how can one make oneself as tall as possible or as small as possible?

Time

Reaction to fast and slow accompaniment through corresponding movements; accelerando and ritardando (only with the help of imaginative stimuli).
Recognising and converting accompanying rhythms into walking, running and skipping.

an uneven number of bars; one should aim for uninterrupted and precise transitions from one type of movement to the other. Change from non-locomotor movements without transfer of weight to various types of locomotion; e.g. draw a figure of eight with one or both arms in the air, following this by stepping an eight out on the floor. Combined step motifs using change step, step and close, cross-over step in different directions, tempi and kinds of metre, in combination with simple walking, running, skipping or bouncing.

small circle (quavers).
Alternate between movement on the spot and in locomotion, e.g. swaying with transfer of weight forwards and backwards, feet one in front of the other, increasing this until it becomes a swinging, forward run.
Combination of steps as for age range 2; add change step with intermediate skip. Polka steps and the simple waltz step used in Ländler. Possibly also simple step forms from popular dances, folk dances and social dances.

The describing of different figures in various sizes (circle, square, figure of eight): in the air or on the floor, alone or in a group (keep changing the leader).
Orientation in the room; middle, edge, corners, diagonal; even spacing; formation of two circles of approximately the same size.
Directions: forwards — backwards, side — side, up — down; these concepts to be combined with tasks using gestures as well as locomotion.

As for age range 2; add quick formation of various figures and group formations (from semi-circle up to three equally-sized circles, rows, position along the diagonal); alternation between individual movement paths and those in the group (with certain space-related tasks). Change of direction and front while moving on the spot and in locomotion; confident performance of the contrasts high — low, narrow — wide, large — small, forwards — backwards. Conscious application of all worked out aspects of space.

As for age range 1; add reaction to sudden and gradual transitions.
Recognition of basic accompanying rhythms as in age range 1; add change step; the picking up of a certain rhythmic motif and its carrying out through individual corresponding movement solutions.

As for age range 2; add the performance of changes of tempo also without accompaniment.
Reaction to different kinds of time, also to changes of time in regular recurrence; free conversion of simple and more difficult rhythms to an accompaniment, performance also

165

Dynamics

The reaction to "loud" and "soft" passages in the accompaniment, e.g. by walking on the whole foot or the ball (this solution must not become a rule); varied energy content in strong, tense movements or softer, more careful ones (e.g. energetic bouncing and soft rolling of a ball).

Forming groups

Real partner work is not yet appropriate for this age group but simple reaction exercises for adaptation to others should be tried.

Forming groups behind an appointed "leading-child", frequent changes of leader; from the movement in a large group pairs should be formed; after a brief period of free movement find the same partner again.

Motivate partner work with the help of equipment.

Timbre
Articulation
Character of the music

Reaction to various instruments. (e.g. short, sharp movements to the sound of the wood block, turning to the shaking of the maracas, slow sinking down to the floor and rising up again to the long reverberation of the cymbal). The choice of movement is left to each individual child. Differences in pitch may indicate change of direction, change of partner, etc.

Group formations and holdings
Space formations and movement paths

The basic formation for this age range is the circle that also includes the teacher. The movement proceeds anticlockwise or clockwise as well as to the centre and back again.

Pairs, with and without holding hands; chains with everyone holding hands, or

Conscious recognition of time units with an even and an uneven number of beats in a bar.

without accompaniment.

As for age range 1; enriched by a more developed dynamic capacity for expression; partner exercises with varied energy effort corresponding to the dynamics of the accompaniment, but also without accompaniment. Working with the help of equipment.

As for age range 2; add finer dynamic gradings (piano, mezzoforte, forte), performed through varied tension, mainly in gesture movements.
Reaction to regular or sudden accents.

As for age range 1; add change of partners while walking, running, jumping; partner work with equipment and instruments; individual tasks can be carried out each time with a new partner, others always with the same (e.g. question and answer with percussion instruments played while dancing); mirror-image exercises.

As for age range 2; change of partners during a movement phrase; changing leadership of a partnership affecting space direction. "Blind" exercises as tasks with a partner or in a group, with changes of leader.
More complex mirror-image exercises (mimed or abstract).

As for age range 1; enriched in all cases by the use of several instruments; differences in articulation in the accompanying music should be reflected in the children's movement reaction. The character of the music may motivate dancing to it or listening.

More varied responses both to the different tone qualities and to the different ways of striking each individual instrument. Reaction to legato and staccato, to the elements of musical form and to the character of the pieces of music used in the lesson.
The setting of individual tasks can here be made by individual children as well as by the teacher.

Circles, also inner and outer circles moving in contrary motion; rows, chains; free, also asymmetrical formations; standing one behind the other, or in the gap between two others; in groups of two and three.
Ways of holding should be tried out

Semi-circle, circle, double circle, rows (opposite one another, one behind the other, or in the gap between two others); chains, chains of pairs, squares, wedge formation, free and asymmetrical formations. (The place of an individual within the group can be main-

both hands on shoulders or on waist of the one in front.

Ways of holding are discovered through trial and error, the most suitable are various ways of linking with one hand or arm.

Movement accompaniment

Accompanying while dancing by means of sound gestures, claves, sleigh bells and tambours.

Accompanying the dance of other children using the above sounds.

Add the simplest ostinati on barred percussion, bass drum or timpani.

Melodic accompaniment through children's singing or teacher's recorder playing. Accompaniment through spoken texts and simple songs using note range of from three to seven notes; rhythmic pulse accompaniment or the simplest motifs using crotchets and quavers and, at the end of a phrase, minims as well. Dividing the children into two groups, one accompanying, the other moving, now and again one child's solo accompaniment.

by the children according to the movement being made (with one hand, both hands, crossed hands, hands on shoulder or on waist, linking arms); changing holds while turning.

tained or changed).

Ways of holding, according to the movement, apart or close; simple changes of hold within the course of a movement.

Accompanying while dancing as for age range 1; add small percussion instruments such as finger cymbals, wood blocks, tambourines, maracas, sleigh bell wristlets (worn also on the ankle). Accompany the dancing of other children as for age range 1; add more complex ostinati as well as simple melodies on barred percussion; perhaps include children with elementary instrumental ability on recorder and piano (also four-hand duet) or other instruments.

Accompaniment through spoken texts and heptatonic songs (major and minor); rhythmic accompaniment using crotchets, quavers, minims and dotted rhythms; melodic improvisation still predominantly pentatonic; the accompaniment still mainly follows the basic rhythm of the movement, partial deviations from the movement rhythm are nevertheless already possible; attention should be paid to clear starts and precise endings.

Solo accompaniment to the movement of a partner or the whole group; similarly accompaniment in smaller groups (mostly through an already known piece that has been worked at or a song with instrumental accompaniment).

Accompanying while dancing as for age range 2; more frequent inclusion of recorders for quieter movement.

Accompanying other children's dancing on percussion instruments (also bongos and timpani), barred percussion, recorders, perhaps plucked and bowed string instruments, piano, gramophone record or recorded tape (in special cases also a recording of music made by the group themselves).

Spoken texts, unison and part songs (also in foreign languages), major – minor, now and then also in church modes; rhythmic accompaniment with all note values given for age range 2; add semiquavers and triplets, rhythmic deviations from the movement rhythm. Solo accompaniment (mainly on bongos, also recorders), as well as accompaniment provided by a small orchestra (prepared music corresponding to dance forms).

Movement composition

Texts: Counting rhymes, knee-riding songs, successions of names, verses, finger-play rhymes (except for the last one, to be used mainly for group games).

Songs: Group games, the simplest ring games, (singing games), action songs with mimetic content.

Rhythmic studies: With sound gestures and small percussion instruments; partner and group tasks; mostly based upon a text that can also serve as an accompaniment; prelude or postlude to a song; traditional children's games as well as inventing new ones.

Instrumental pieces: At first only in the simplest form; more experienced children play melodic ostinati on barred percussion, the teacher or a particularly gifted child the melody.

Descriptive play, scenes from fairy tales: A continuous form may be created from songs, texts and small instrumental pieces.

Individual parts should be developed from improvisation since the "rehearsal" of longer sequences is not suitable for children in this age group.

Texts: Counting-out rhymes, nonsense rhymes, sayings, riddles; also simple, short rhymes and sayings in a foreign language, the children's own verses set to individual or group compositions.

Songs: Dance-songs as communal dances in traditional form or in a form newly created by the children with help from the teacher; action songs that depict a scenic event that can be performed in dance or mime for scenic improvisation and for a musically fixed composition in strophic form.

Rhythmic studies: With or without the help of texts; with sound gestures or small percussion instruments played while dancing (from the improvisation of questions and answers to rhythmic rondos and simple canons).

Instrumental pieces: In the most varied instrumentation (barred percussion, recorders, other percussion); ternary form, round, canon etc; simple performance of the movement when the music is complicated; the accompanying instruments should at times be included in the space used for dancing; dancers and musicians exchange places.

Mimetic play, scenes from fairy tales: Extension of the action songs to larger, connected scenes.

Individual compositions: All children work simultaneously but independently on one or more (also freely chosen) themes. Suitable for this are themes from nature (animals, wind, water, plants), from technology (pendulum, machines), from fairy tales, from everyday life or from children's reading matter; compositions with musical instruments (percussion instruments, recorders) or equipment (ropes, balls, balloons, hoops).

Compositions done in twos or small groups: The themes are similar to those of the individual compositions, but with simultaneous contrasting movements added to the solo factor.

Texts: Presentation of riddles, proverbs (also those in a foreign language), sayings, short poems.

Songs: Dance songs and singing games (the dance form is abstract, mostly similar to a folk dance, possibly with variations in the individual verses), action songs.

Rhythmic studies: changing between solo and tutti; richer in instrumentation and in movement performance; more difficult than age range 2 in the movement rhythms as well as in the variation of striking the instrument.

Instrumental pieces: As for age range 2; the individual parts are more extensive; The corresponding relationship between music and movement should be clearly worked out; besides pieces from Orff-Schulwerk, simple piano pieces that the children can play themselves should be used (e.g. by Bartók, Casella, Kabalevski, Stravinsky), as well as dance music for recorders and other instruments or montages of sounds.

Mimetic play, scenes from fairy tales: The combination of dancing, singing, speaking and playing instruments. More extensive forms can be worked out and performed together by various groups of children or by classes.

Traditional dances: Simple authentic folk-dances, community dances or early court dances, mostly to recorded music.

Part Five
Lesson Examples

Age range 1: Four to six years

Inter, mitzy, titzy, tool*

Inter, mitzy, titzy, tool,
Ira, dira, dominu,
Oker, poker, dominoker,
Out goes you.

Instruments and equipment: One clave or bamboo stick for each child, small percussion instruments and a recorder for the teacher.

Nearly all counting-out rhymes have a traditional play form: the children stand in a circle while one of them counts them out in turn until only one remains who then has something special to do (hide himself or look for the others, or be the catcher in a catching game). This familiar activity can be the starting point for a game that includes dance, speech, rhythmic accompaniment and melody.

Plan: The text given above is played several times as a game in the usual way and spoken (or sung) by all the children. Those standing in the circle accompany with clapping (patschen or stamping). The accompaniment most often chosen by children consists of one accent on each word, nevertheless other rhythms should be tried. After a while the rhythm is no longer spoken but just clapped according to its speech rhythm.

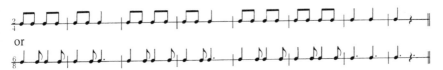

Half the children (group A) take a pair of claves each and sit in a large circle. The children without claves (group B) choose a partner from those who are seated. While group A plays the rhythm of the rhyme each child in group B dances round his partner (walking, running, skipping etc.). On the last beat the dancers take the claves and take over the accompaniment while the others now stand up and do the dancing round their partners.

The Oxford Nursery Rhyme Book, page 111

Theme development: The original form of the counting-out rhyme and the 'abstract' type of game described above can be combined in a rondo form.

A: Wordless game with change of role (see above).

B: All the children stand in a circle, each now with one clave held in front, pointing centre. The child doing the counting now speaks the rhyme, striking the other claves with his own as he goes round the circle one by one. When he comes to the end of the rhyme he dances inside the circle with the child counted "out" to a recorder melody played by the teacher, while the other children improvise a rhythmic accompaniment or dance too.

A: Wordless game with change of role.

C: Counting out as in B this time until about four or five children have been counted "out". As he is counted out each child chooses a percussion instrument from those that have been set out somewhere in the circle (bass drum, maracas, jingles, tambour etc.) one instrument being reserved for the child who has been doing the counting – the last child to be counted out is allowed to conduct the orchestra. The dance to the recorder melody is now danced by all the remaining children and the "orchestra" accompany quietly to the end.

A: Return to wordless game with change of role.

Obviously one need only use one of the versions mentioned above. Motivation for play and for repetition can always arise when a particular task that all the children like performing is being offered, (e.g. being allowed to suggest a game or to choose one, conducting, being allowed to try something quite new for the first time, etc.). The decision can be made through the counting out game within whose well-known form a new task is given every time a child is 'out'.

Suggestions for variation: Improvise melodies to the given text or to that of some other counting-out rhyme; find simple accompaniments on barred percussion instruments; take up a particular dance form demonstrated by a child or by the teacher; try out the setting of precise movement tasks (only skipping, only turning, only travelling to the centre of the circle and back, etc.).

One to make ready *

One to make ready,
And two to prepare;
Good luck to the rider,
And away goes the mare.

This example can serve, as do knee-riding and other rhymes about horses, to stimulate locomotion. The objection of some educationalists that horses and riding and everything that relates to it is no more a living part of the experience of the city child is unfortunately true insofar as direct contact is concerned. Experiences, undoubtedly of a secondary nature, that exercise children's

The Oxford Nursery Rhyme Book, page 77

imagination are nevertheless to be found on television, and in films and books. In addition this theme is particularly suitable for experiences in space, time, dynamics and communication.

Introduction of the theme: Some talking about horses; the children contribute their own experiences; reference to television animal programmes; children's books; horseguards etc.

Opinions are given: horses move very fast but also at an easy pace, they walk, trot and gallop. Some are packhorses carrying heavy loads, others can perform clever tricks (e.g. the Lipizzaner of the Viennese riding school), others run in races for betting and are ridden by a jockey. Has anyone ever ridden a horse? Do all riders ride in the same way? There will certainly be many other relevant connections in the school situation. Of all that we have discussed what can we try out for ourselves? Who would like to try to move like a wild mustang, a dressage horse, a circus horse or a racehorse?

Setting of tasks: After making the first experiments, showing some examples from them and discussing these, everyone works at some basic techniques.
1) Walk-trot-gallop
All three are practised and the children are encouraged to have a supple, rolling foot action, good elasticity and light but energetic take-off from the floor. The children's attention should be drawn to the difference in the sounds made by the feet (the rhythm of the feet). Who can tell from the accompaniment how the horse is moving, if it is far away or near? (The notation can only, of course, be relative).

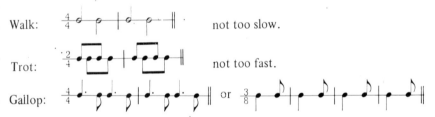

Walk: not too slow.

Trot: not too fast.

Gallop:

2) Movement paths
How do horses move on a street or path (straight ahead, mostly in a straight line)? How do they move in a circus (in a circle, in a figure of eight)? How in a wood (zigzag or in curves, skilfully avoiding all obstacles)?

The wood, the circus arena etc., could perhaps be indicated through the strategic placing of various objects, or of children. The children learn and practise with concrete objects, but these can soon be omitted and space orientation is achieved through the imagination.
3) How do horses move together? A herd of mustangs or animals on pasture land move in a disorganised mass with those that run best at the front. Circus horses move at an exact distance beside or behind one another, which is much more difficult than rushing along in a crowd. How can one represent a carriage with two or four horses?

177

Theme development: After practising together each child now chooses once more the role that he likes best. Perhaps several make a group of race horses, others want to try out an idea about a circus, a third group forms a coach and horses. The "loners" can think up an individual theme.

Once the children have experimented for a while in small groups and the teacher has helped and advised the groups, then the various ideas can be brought together into a simple form.

A herald, announcer or all the bystanders call out:

One to make ready,   (On \ a beat on the bass drum)

And two to prepare;   (On \ a beat on the wood block)

Good luck to the rider,   (On \ a beat on a tambour or a clap)

And away goes the mare.   (On \ a beat on a big cymbal)

One small group or a single child now show what they have tried out. Following this, different children can go to the instruments or can accompany the rhyme with sound gestures and we then have another example. The verse can be repeated as often as necessary (variations: one voice alone, all voices, spoken, sung) accompanied with different instruments or simply with sound gestures, in different rhythms, e.g.:

or

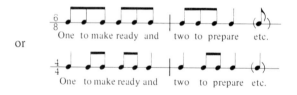

Other texts can lead to different tasks or forms; for further suggestions see The Oxford Nursery Rhyme Book pp. 12-15.

The tone colour of sounds as a stimulation to movement

This example shows how reaction to different colours of sound can be used as a stimulus to movement and how, with the addition of small percussion instruments a simple form can be made.

Movement material: The children choose movements that correspond to the sound of individual instruments, the movement material arising out of the children's spontaneous choice.

Instruments: Tambour, maracas, hanging cymbal and wood block.

178

The movement follows the resonance of the accompanying sound.

Preparatory exercises: With young children this exercise can be introduced through a story that will act as an imaginative stimulus.

The children stand, spread out in the room, each with enough space around him. The teacher now begins to play on a wood block, e.g.

The children move stiffly, almost like marionettes; they walk with sudden, wooden steps or move only their arms and legs on the spot.

Another instrument is tried: the maracas. Through making small circular movements the teacher plays it in such a way that a continuous sound is heard. The children move quite quickly to this, they trip along, turn on the spot or wriggle with their arms and legs.

The next instrument is the tambour. The children are familiar with the continuous quavers played on it from a previous lesson and they run or skip to this.

Finally the teacher gives a beat upon the cymbal. As a stimulation to movement this sound is new to the children and they react with some surprise, stretch or make themselves quite small, make wide gestures with their arms and all around their trunk. Each time a new instrument is played the teacher names it and the children repeat the name.

To recover everyone sits on the floor, head on knees and arms around them, the eyes closed. One instrument after the other is played with its particular motif and the children listen and name the instrument in each case.

Once the majority of the children can distinguish the individual sounds and name the instruments that make them, a discussion takes place as to which movement best suits the individual motifs; some children can show their ideas. Four children are chosen. At a sign from the teacher or from a child each plays one of the instruments. The others have organised themselves into four groups, one group moving to the tambour, one to the maracas, etc. The children playing the instruments should stand as far away as possible so that the others cannot see them. When the sound of an instrument stops then the corresponding group remains still. If the teacher gives the signal to two instrumentalist children at once, then two groups will be moving. After a while the roles are changed.

In a future lesson one can work further with this material and create a simple form out of it.

Outline of the forms:

1) Each child dances for himself alone. The accompaniment changes irregularly from one instrument to another. Each child finds his own solution according to previous experience.

2) It may be decided, for instance, that at the sound of the wood block only the hands will dance, with the maracas only the feet. At first two sounds will be enough, later a third or fourth can be added. The children decide for themselves how they will react to each sound.

3) Small group. As for number 2) the teacher plays the same motifs on one instrument after the other and the children do the movements they have decided on for each sound. This is a reaction exercise rather than one concerned with the characteristic sound of each instrument.

4) The children stand in four circles. In the centre of each circle there is a child with an instrument. In turn the circles now begin to move to their respective instruments. The change from one to the next can be shown by the teacher or a child; it can also be left to the judgement of the four instrumentalists.

The following is another possibility:
   All the instruments are around the teacher. She either plays them herself or she invites a small group of players to help her. The children form as many circles as they wish — double circles are also possible. Two beats on the cymbal are heard: when they hear the first the children slowly make themselves small. When they can no longer hear any sound their foreheads are touching the floor. On the second beat they stretch upwards again just as slowly. The second instrument to be heard is the wood block: all remain on one spot and move only arms and head like a marionette. The third instrument to sound is the tambour: they skip or run forwards in their circles until they hear the maracas, when they stop and turn round on the spot. At the end they hear the cymbal once more and sink slowly to the floor.
   After several weeks, when this game is familiar, one can try to develop a simple, two-part exercise. The children form double circles that move simultaneously but to different motifs.

*Wee Willie Winkie**

Wee Willie Winkie runs through the town,
Upstairs and downstairs in his nightgown,
Rapping at the window, crying through the lock,
Are the children all in bed, for now it's eight o'clock?

   In this example a dance-scene presentation is stimulated by the story of Wee Willie Winkie, who saw to it that all children were in bed at a proper time.

Introduction of the theme: The teacher brings a child's drawing of Wee Willie Winkie, or she (or a child) talks about him. The children try now to describe him with words, perhaps with pictures or through movements. Suddenly there are many Wee Willie Winkies who are traversing the streets and slipping past the houses in very different ways. Some are tripping along and some go from house to house in great leaps. They look through windows, keyholes and doors, slip, run and jump to the next etc.

The Oxford Nursery Rhyme Book, page 36.

Preparatory exercises: The story is concerned with Wee Willie Winkie, the town and the children. In the first experiment the star role was important, but now the appearance of the town must be considered. Several children will be able to represent a house. They try to make large and small houses, some with a tower, others with many small windows through which Wee Willie Winkie can peep. Inside the houses there must be room for the children in the story. Some are already in bed, others are looking out of the windows, but some are not yet at home and are running quickly through the streets as Wee Willie Winkie comes along. Apart from depicting the scene the moment for introducing accompaniment to the movement has to be prepared. One child plays the part of Wee Willie Winkie and the others try to accompany his movements appropriately. (At first it is best for them to close their eyes so that they can listen more attentively to the sound of his movements). What instrument can one use? Which best suits a Wee Willie Winkie who stamps, or one who slips and trips along? Should one play loudly or softly, fast or slow and how can one alter the tone quality of an instrument? Such questions give scope for considerable experiment.

Finally, the song should be practised together with some rhythmic or melodic accompaniment (see Music for Children (Murray) I p.7 and Wee Willie Winkie p.4, both in the Orff-Schulwerk series). When everything has been practised, the individual parts can be put together into some kind of sequence.

Outline of the form: One group of children are musicians and singers, another represents the houses; some are the children inside and outside the houses and a soloist plays Wee Willie Winkie.

As an introduction Wee Willie Winkie is heard coming in the distance. Some children accompany him with instruments or sounds that match his movements (e.g. scratching and stroking a tambour for a Wee Willie Winkie who creeps, short sounds on a wood block for one who trips along with small steps, triangle accents for a jumping Wee Willie Winkie). When he gets to the town the "music" group sing the song (with accompaniment) that tells how he goes from house to house. When the song comes to an end the individual accompaniment starts once more. Wee Willie Winkie can, of course, speak or sing himself and ask at every house whether all the children are at home and in bed. The houses (the children that represent them) give an answer.

Since all the children will obviously want to play the solo part there must be frequent changes of role. Representing the houses is rather tiring and the concentration of the children concerned can only be maintained for a short time. It is also desirable that everyone should be once in the music group and another time in the acting group. Care must be taken that the children do not imitate one another but that every house and every Wee Willie Winkie should find their own character and movement.

This old man

This old man,
he played two,
he played nick nack
on my shoe, etc.

This old man   he played one,   he played nick nack   on my drum;

nick nack pad-dy whack, give a dog a bone, this old man came roll-ing home.

Well known children's songs should not always be danced only in the traditional form or in a fixed form provided by the teacher, but should provide stimulation for individual improvisation and spontaneous composition. Through simple instrumental accompaniments the children's activity is supported and intensified.

Preparatory exercises: Who knows the song with so many verses about the strange old man? Perhaps the children can invent new verses with different rhymes? The teacher could perhaps accompany the singing with simple chords on a guitar. In any case all the children can accompany with sound gestures or with small percussion instruments, e.g.

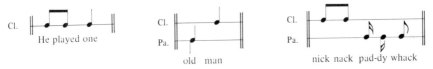

Cl.   He played one   Cl.   Pa.   old man   Cl.   Pa.   nick nack pad-dy whack

The individual rhythmic ostinati can also be played on various instruments and can be combined with one another. Some children, rather than playing the ostinati, will prefer to play longer rhythmic phrases. If there is a bass drum it can be put into the centre of the space, every child being given a turn on it as "this old man", accompanying the singing of the others.

How can one dance to this singing and playing? All try dancing simultaneously around the drum as a child plays it. Perhaps one child or another wants to show how he has danced and the others try to copy him. (At first it is most important that every child just dances, regardless of whether he imitates the others or not. Later, there should be as many different suggestions as possible.) When the children are not very inspired the teacher must stimulate new ideas through the way she sets tasks, e.g.:

— Who can skip in a circle round the drummer?
— Who can dance only with arms and hands without allowing their feet to leave the floor?

183

- Who can dance on one leg only?
- Who can dance with quick steps towards the drummer and away again?
- Who can hold hands with a partner and dance round and round one another?
- Who can find funny steps to make with heels and toes?
- Who can take big jumps between their steps?

Outline of the form: The children sit around but not too close to the drum and sing and accompany the first verse. One child plays the old man and dances round the drum. When the verse is over he improvises alone on the drum.

In the second verse another child dances the first half of the verse alone, in the second half he and the first child dance together, repeating the kind of movement shown by the second child. All the rest are singing and accompanying. The second child now plays his improvisation alone on the drum.

In the third verse a third child takes part. He makes up his dance in the first half and it is taken up by the other two in the second half, etc.

In every verse then, a new child takes part who may first dance his own kind of steps that the others have to imitate and then he may play his own improvisation on the drum.

If necessary the form can be simplified; in which case, in the second half of each verse the other dancing children skip round the drum in a circle holding hands. This omits the difficulty of imitating demonstrated movements.

Age range 2: Six to eight years

Tweedledum and Tweedledee

This short nursery rhyme, quoted by Lewis Carroll in his "Alice through the looking glass", suggests a dance presentation and stimulates the invention of one's own "theatre music". This theme is particularly suitable for a teaching team (dance, music, art) through which the three main fields of scenic production, musical composition and the provision of costumes, properties or pictures can be realised. The relationship to Alice's story does not have to be preserved, it exists in its own right as a nursery rhyme and as such can be treated freely.

Tweedledum and Tweedledee
Agreed to have a battle
For Tweedledum said Tweedledee
Had spoiled his nice new rattle.
Just then flew by a monstrous crow
As big as a tar barrel,
Which frightened both the heroes so
They quite forgot their quarrel.

Preparatory exercises:
1) How the unfolding of the story should be presented, what movement material should be used, and the musical ideas — these should come mainly from the children; the teacher should help rather than lead.
2) As far as is possible every child should at some time have the chance to play one of the leading roles. In some cases, therefore, several groups can try out their solutions simultaneously. Where there is enough time the roles (and the instruments) played can be changed around.
3) After the first, working-out stage, various suggestions for the presentation of one role can be shown and one or more of the clearest versions chosen.
4) Should the various versions turn out to be rather similar, the teacher should not then suggest or demonstrate movements that are too precise but should rather describe the character more precisely (e.g. the crow flaps its wings awkwardly and threateningly in ever narrowing circles round the terrified "heroes").
5) The most important rule for the fight is that the contestants are not allowed to touch each other. A mock fight is very much more difficult to do than a real tussle.
6) If the group is very large, small groups that only play the Tweedledum, the

Tweedledee or the crow music can be formed. Apart from this each of the two heroes can be accompanied by a retinue, friends or a gang so that thirty children or more can be given something to do.

7) It is important that every child is given as many of the different tasks as possible, so that the musicians also try acting roles and those that are miming are also involved in the production of the necessary properties.

Planning discussion:

This can be introductory or it can be continued at a specific time. Many questions, that should help the children to plan and consider how to present the story scenically and musically, are asked and discussed, and then tried out. This experimental stage, which should produce as much "raw material" as possible, will be continually enriched through new questions and stimulation from children or teacher, e.g.:

Who were Tweedledum and Tweedledee? — What do they look like, how do you imagine them to be? — How do they move? — What instruments or sound will be suitable for the crow and how shall we produce such sounds? — How can we make the battle really exciting? — What should the two of them do at the end, run away in terror, collapse on the floor from shock or what else could they do? etc., etc.

According to inspiration the children can produce several different versions in which the poem

a) acts as a stimulus but is not actually used;

b) is spoken by a narrator describing the story.

c) is partly spoken, partly sung, and possibly recorded on tape to be added to the final performance. This latter possibility is particularly suitable for somewhat older children who are more interested in both the technicalities of recording and in the establishing of a fixed version, rather than in spontaneous improvising of new versions every time.

One of the many possible versions might be outlined as follows:

1) Entry of Tweedledum and retinue (Tweedledum music)

2) Entry of Tweedledee and retinue (Tweedledee music)

3) Battle of the two heroes and their followers

4) Appearance of the monstrous crow

5) Flight of the heroes

Suggestions for presentation

Tweedledum: Perhaps he is very fat and can only walk slowly with a rather straddling gait. He also has to keep pausing for breath after only a few steps. He is proud and vain and proceeds from one side to the other inviting admiration.
Movement: slow, interrupted, broad, heavy, puffed-up.

Tweedledee: If the children have decided that they are twins then one can present a mirror image of the other and imitate the other's movements exactly. Another possibility would be that Tweedledee is in every way the exaggerated opposite of

	Tweedledum and therefore tall, thin, quick and hectic, shambling, restless.
Crow:	Can be played by one child or by several, in which case the monstrous nature of the bird can be more clearly conveyed. Head, beak and wings are important. Perhaps a large piece of dark cloth could enhance the effect.
Retinues:	The movements of the followers should be as like those of their leader as possible.

Music: This can be extremely simple and only needs to support the action with sounds that are made vocally, or with instruments (including unconventional ones!) or it can be a carefully prepared and developed group improvisation or composition.

Three motifs are needed:

1) Tweedledum — Low-pitched sounds, bass xylophone, 'cello pizzicato, low-pitched drums, low humming.

2) Tweedledee — Higher, shriller sounds, wind instruments, brighter-sounding percussion, distorted voice sounds.

3) Crow — Startling, penetrating sounds, glissandi of vocal clusters, possibly the flexible plastic tubes that make a wailing sound when whirled round and round, cymbals, etc.

It is by no means necessary that the music be in strict metre; on the contrary it can be largely without metre and quite sparsely used.

Let the piper call the tune — La Rotta

The chief character here, the musician who can influence others through his playing, is known from Orpheus, through the Pied Piper of Hamlin to the present day pop stars. The teacher herself can find a simple story that will stimulate a more elaborate presentation.

Story: Something like this — It has become widely known that there is a young musician, or a group of players who through their music make everyone dance and feel happy. But not all the people want this music. There are some who say that it makes a noise and causes disturbance, that it encourages people not to go to work and that it cannot be allowed. To make these tiresome dissidents change their minds the 'fans' make use of a chorus of speakers who chant: 'Let the piper call the tune'. While the dissidents still refuse to give way and are barricading the square, the musicians have meanwhile turned up in another place, near at hand. They are playing and everyone, finally also the dissidents, is compelled to dance.

Recorder music such as dances from the middle ages; a South American dance; for young adolescents recorder pop music such as that of Anderson and Jethro Tull can serve as a musical stimulus to the dance.

Preparatory exercises: This material can be so modified that it can also be used with older children or adolescents. Both the music and the style of dancing must be suitable to the requirements of the situation.

The theme can be developed over several sessions, for each section tackled can place the main emphasis on a different aspect.
1) Dance improvisation
2) Development of the choral speaking
3) Working out a dance form

1) Dance improvisation
Different aspects can be emphasised (see Chapter on Improvisation p. 140) i.e. an utterly free, spontaneous dancing without regard to form, partner or movement task. This freeing from all restriction is necessary for some children, while others feel themselves rather more inhibited by so much freedom. For this reason simple tasks should soon be given:
a) Improvising with a partner; changing from leader to follower and vice versa, looking for a new partner without breaking the flow, taking over the new partner's movement . . . .
b) Trying out various movement possibilities; how can one dance mainly with the arms and hands? What kinds of ingenious steps or hops can one discover, what kinds of movement or floor patterns? . . . . .
c) Coinciding with the musical structure; finding clear endings, recognising repetitions and making them, possibly including sound gestures as a rhythmic accompaniment . . . .
At first only one aspect at a time is taken into consideration, but by the end of the lesson it should be possible for most of the children to make use of the movements they have thought out and, with a partner, create a dance that corresponds to the form of the music that has been chosen.

2) Development of the choral speaking
The children make suggestions as to how the text can be spoken. The teacher should help to clarify and organise rather than provide a finished form. For instance:

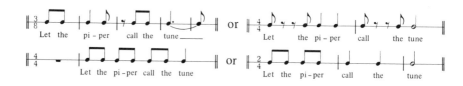

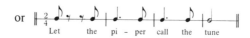

Eventually a version in more than one part develops out of the various suggestions.

188

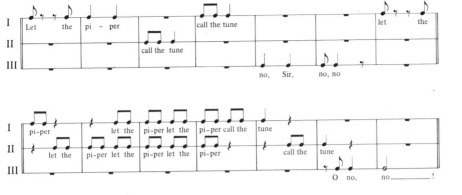

This simple speech chorus can be staged, or at least some production indicated, but the words must be clearly spoken and rhythmically precise before any production is attempted.

The production might take the following form: The dissidents form a solid chain with linked arms. The others approach in two groups with the intention of breaking through the chain. It is easier for children to move when they do not have to think about a text, and their movement will be freer and more intensive. Before the chain can be broken, however, the piper and his drummer appear from another side and start to play an introduction that entices everyone in his direction.

3) Working out a simple dance form

The musical example given here is called 'La Rotta' a fourteenth century dance:

This melody, with its dance-like character and clear form, will be too difficult for six to eight-year-old children to play on the recorder. The teacher will therefore have to take the part of the piper, or one of the children mimes the part (without instrument) while the tune is reproduced on a tape recorder.

Two different motifs are prepared for the A and B parts.

A) Skipping evenly in a chain with stamps at the end of each phrase;
B) An improvisation and its repetition.

As a preparation for the first the children need to become secure in their ability to form a chain or a circle and to change easily from the one formation to the other. They can be given this experience in the form of a warming-up exercise at the beginning of the lesson, first by walking, later with other forms of locomotion. For the second motif accurate observation is needed so that a precise repetition can be made.

A part   A child leads a chain in a wide curve round the musicians; by the end of the first part the chain has become a circle. The step material consists of even skips with, according to the skill of the children, stamps at the end of each phrase:

B part   A soloist dances around or with the musicians (four bars), and his improvisation is repeated by the group. At the repeat of the B part a second soloist improvises and is again imitated by everyone else. The group might accompany the soloist with sound gestures. Should the whole dance be repeated several times the drummer can decide who is to lead the chain again by standing in front of him at the end of the B part.

The three individual sections, each of which forms a complete unit, can be combined to form a larger sequence, though it is certainly more important to maintain the play character than to have a trouble-free transition from one scene to the next.

Rhythmic canon with names

A child's remark, that people from other lands have strange sounding names that are sometimes spelt in a similar way to those that are familiar to us and yet pronounced very differently, could be a starting point for this canon. From this idea we can make a rhythmic game with the names of people from other lands.

Movement material: Stamping, clapping and patschen in various combinations, on the spot and while travelling; walking and skipping evenly (double bounce). The movements of this canon are deliberately kept simple. The attention should rather be focussed on canonic form.

Preparatory exercises: To warm up the children skip in pairs holding inside hands. Those standing on the right lead first and the others adjust to them. At an acoustic signal the roles are reversed. The teacher accompanies on a tambour in a skipping rhythm (see p. 86). After the children have exchanged roles several times the accompaniment changes to quavers. The take-off is now no longer accented and the resulting movement is a double bounce (two even hops on each foot alternately) while travelling. This preparatory exercise should be tried at the beginning of several lessons so that the children learn to know the difference between the usual accompaniment for skipping and that for even skipping (double bounce) and how to make the difference in movement. The next stage tackles the alternation of walking and double bounce in phrases of equal length. Exercise in pairs: Each child that stands on the right (No. 1) walks, those on the left (No. 2) remain standing and clap. Then the 'twos' walk and the 'ones' clap. In the same way the change between walking and double bounce is practised and a simple movement canon occurs: The 'ones' walk; as they begin the double bounce the 'twos' start walking.

The next stage is to collect some names. When the children's supply of foreign names is exhausted the teacher can help with suggestions, preferably from stories and books familiar to the children, e.g.:

♩ : Fritz, Hans, Sven, Juan, Pierre, Paul.

♩ ♩ : Eva, Birgit, Katja, Astrid, Gustav, Heidi, Carlos, Wilhelm, Leila, Carmen, Pedro.

♩ ♩ ♩ : Manuel, Leonhart, Giacomo, Fatima, Frantisek, Dominique, Raffael.

♩ ♩ ♩ ♩ : Isabella, Katarina, Cleopatra, Leonardo.

♩ | ♩ ♩ : Therese, Ulrike, Elias, Susanna, Gerardo, Orlando.

♩ | ♩ : José, Françoise, Madeleine, Ramón.

These examples can be extended. The names are clapped, stamped, and patsched and practised in various combinations. The rhythms of the names are translated into notation. Finally a form is selected and notated.

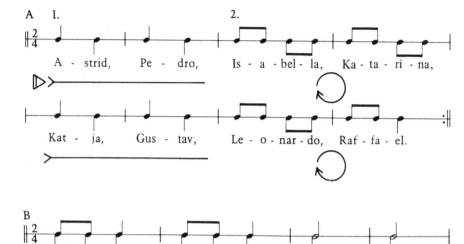

Sequence: The form — A B A — is first practised in unison, A while travelling, B on the spot, A travelling again.

A: The rhythm is clapped while the children walk four steps forwards (two bars), then two bars of double bounce turning on the spot. Each part is repeated. During the A part the children clap quietly.

B: The first two bars are clapped while standing. Then all the children go down quickly onto their right knees and strike the two minims with their hands on the floor. The rising and kneeling must be quick and supple (some advance practice may be necessary).

A: As above, with repeat.

Work at the canon can begin once the children know and can perform the whole sequence securely in unison. It is at first advisable for the teacher, and later some of the more secure children, to take over the second entry. It can then be tried in two equal groups.

Possible group arrangements are: several rows, each child standing behind the gap made between two children in the row in front, also in wedge shape or in two rows facing one another but some distance apart (at the repetition of the A part the children do a half turn and walk away from one another).

192

$\triangledown$ = 1st entry

$\blacktriangledown$ = 2nd entry

Kaleidoscope

The optical toy, known to most children as a kaleidoscope, is the stimulus for this experimental dance game. One can buy various types in toy shops and stores. One can use them all but the most effective are those that contain small pieces of brightly coloured glass, that, when shaken, fall into a particular pattern that is then made symmetrical through reflection. The presentation of this them follows the different learning stages described on page 44.

1) Motivation – Setting the problem: The children play with their kaleidoscopes, turning and shaking them so that they are always seeing new patterns. While doing this they voice their observations, e.g.: ". . when I move all the little bits of glass fall about all over the place, but when I keep still, so do they;" ". . in every corner the pattern is exactly the same;" ". . they fall from one pattern into the other;" ". . I can see eight of those red stars and each one has a yellow blob beside it" etc. Most of the children have recognised movement as the opposite of stillness as well as the properties of symmetrical order.

The teacher's question as to whether the children can create this effect themselves with their own bodies leads to:

2) Action – Experimental phase: Some of the observations are taken up. Can the children, like the pieces of glass, stop suddenly and hold their position in absolute stillness?Then, when the accompaniment begins again, start a new movement? Perhaps they should sometimes touch one another (the glass pieces are also touching one another most of the time). How can one bring it about that a pattern is simultaneously repeated four or more times? (Suggestion: When four children, though moving in different ways, take up and maintain the same end position at a given signal).

All these questions and suggestions are tried out in practice and various versions are shown.

3) Reflection – Choice: In a short discussion the most suitable solutions are chosen and some additional guidelines given:

The area on which the children are working should be severely limited in order to restrict locomotion to the advantage of gesture.

At every pause or position of stillness a new point of contact must be found (e.g. forehead, elbows, heels, knees etc.). To do this one can sometimes lie, kneel, sit or stand.

The transition from one position to a new one is very important, just as important as the position itself and should be executed inventively, evenly and without interruption. Where the time available is very short the most direct way has to to be found; when the accompaniment allows more time, detours and flourishes can be invented.

4) Action – Working out – Differentiation – Optimum performance: Each group (of four children) decides upon the order of points of contact and position (e.g. lying on the floor, the toes touch; standing, the elbows touch; kneeling, the heels touch in the air; finally, standing, the heads touch). The length of each transition is established and remains constant, provided by the teacher using such sounds as the rustling of maracas, a drum roll, rubbing a tambour skin with the palm of the hand. Not a metrically structured accompaniment, in fact, but one with dynamic rise and fall. The pauses between should not last too long since children of this age have a limited concentration span.

The sequences, at first chosen freely and then retained, possibly further refined through suggestions from child or teacher, are now practised and brought to as much clarity and precision as possible. Finally the individual versions are shown.

5) Reflection – Affirmation – Making connections – Further developments: As a result of this example the experiences gained can be discussed again, i.e.:
– Contrast between flowing movement and held position.
– Short phrase producing direct paths, longer one resulting in indirect paths containing detours and flourishes.
– Possible introduction of the concept "symmetry".
– Similarities between the actual kaleidoscope patterns and those made by the children with their bodies.

What new ideas result from these considerations? How could the game be changed or enlarged? e.g.:
– Using various instruments or sources of sound for each phrase
– Introducing material objects
– Painting kaleidoscope pictures

Carillon de Vendôme*

This French song provides an example of how a song in a foreign language can be used. The text should not be too difficult to learn. In some cases it would be possible to use only the first verse and to keep repeating it. There are opportunities in this song for the combination of a folk dance type of ring dance, together with the mimed presentation of individual characters (king, society lady, farmer, horseman, jester, workman, drummer) such as one sees on old chiming clocks where figures come out and dance when certain hours are struck.

*Orff-Schulwerk, *Music for Children*, Vol. 3, p.22 Schott, London.

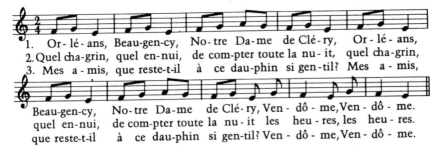

1. Or-lé-ans, Beau-gen-cy, No-tre Da-me de Clé-ry, Or-lé-ans,
2. Quel cha-grin, quel en-nui, de com-pter toute la nu-it, quel cha-grin,
3. Mes a-mis, que reste-t-il à ce dau-phin si gen-til? Mes a-mis,

Beau-gen-cy, No-tre Da-me de Clé-ry, Ven-dô-me, Ven-dô-me.
quel en-nui, de com-pter toute la nu-it les heu-res, les heu-res.
que reste-t-il à ce dau-phin si gen-til? Ven-dô-me, Ven-dô-me.

Movement material: Simple step combinations of running and skipping in a circle or in pairs. The presentation of the individual figures arises out of improvisation.

Instruments and apparatus: The setting to be found in Orff-Schulwerk, Volume Three requires glockenspiels, metallophone, glasses and a violoncello or guitar. This instrumentation best represents the characteristics of a chiming clock, though other instruments can of course be used. If available a small platform, stage blocks or tables placed together can be used for the figures, possibly also some stage properties.

Preparatory exercises: As an introduction the teacher tells of a time in French history when, after a battle, only the towns of Orléans, Beaugency and Cléry remained in the possession of the Dauphin. She also tells of a certain town hall clock on which, at a certain hour, figures come out and dance. Perhaps she could find pictures of clocks of this kind. In England, working examples are to be seen in Wells Cathedral, and in London in the British Museum and outside the stores of Fortnum and Mason and Libertys.

The individual figures will naturally arouse the most interest in the children. The improvised characterisation of these different roles offers a good opportunity to work out a version of this song. How will a king with mantle, crown and sceptre hold himself and how will he walk? How does the court jester jump about with his cap and bells? How does the society lady carry herself? How does one show the tired, depressed carriage of a beggar? What kinds of typical movements can the children find for a farmer, a cobbler, a horseman or a drummer?

Every child chooses a role; he tries to find a posture and a way of moving about that is typical for his character. The speed at which the clockwork revolves has to be established for this will determine the speed of the movements. They decide too whether their character is going to turn as they travel. During this experimentation the teacher or a child plays the melody. If the class is divided into two, one half can sing and play the accompaniment of the song, previously prepared in the music lesson, while the other half works at the characterisations. After a while they change roles. The children select the best versions.

If these preparations have been successful a sequence that hangs together can be tried. Twelve cymbal strokes indicate midday. The clock, represented by a child with cymbal and beater in his hand, should stand above the

Characteristic pose for a
drummer, king, jester and lady.

dancing figures on a further platform or stage block. All the children who are not involved as figures or orchestra come, while the clock strikes, to the centre of the room and group themselves round the platforms representing the clock-tower. Accompanied by the orchestra and the singing of the "onlookers", the figures dance, turning slowly all the time they travel, making movements that are typical for the character concerned. At the end of the verse they stop abruptly. The melody is now played again (but not sung) as an entr'acte, possibly with a different orchestration, and this time it is the onlookers that dance. Some form small circles in threes or fours, others dance alone or in pairs. The movement can remain free and spontaneous, or it can have been chosen by one of the children and practised beforehand (e.g. two runs followed by a step-hop: r, l, r, r; l, r, l, l).

For the second verse the onlookers stop dancing and sing once more while the figures begin their movements again. For the second entr'acte the onlookers form two chains, holding hands and using the same step as before, and are taken by their leaders in various curves around the tower. For the third verse they watch once more, possibly adding a quiet rhythmic accompaniment. During the epilogue the onlookers form two concentric circles holding hands and dancing in opposite directions at an ever increasing speed. Finally the clock strikes, the figures disappear and the people go home.

Outline of the dance:

Prologue: The children come in small groups and collect, like passers-by, around the tower.
First verse: The figures dance, the other children sing and watch the figures.
Entr'acte: The onlookers form small groups of two, three and four that dance together.
Second verse: The figures dance again.
Entr'acte: The onlookers dance in two chains around the tower.
Third verse: The figures dance and the watching children invent accompaniments.
Epilogue: All dance round the tower in two concentric circles until the clock strikes.

Prologue, Entr'actes and Epilogue are played by the instruments, the three verses are sung and accompanied by the instruments.

The figures on the clock tower dance, the visitors watch.

Entr'acte — the onlookers dance.

Age range 3: Eight to ten years

*Dancing**

Booming thundering sound.
The continuous booming of the drum.
Children start moving in stiff movements
A flicking in time movement, arms reaching, feet snapping
Bodies stiff.
The rhythm changes.
Sweeping, swooping, gliding
Relaxed.
Fingers trail through the air.
The drum ceases and movement stops. . .

This poem by a ten year old New Zealand boy gives us a very concrete picture of movement and also contains precise indications for a musical structure. The emphasis here will be on contrasted movement qualities and the related expressive qualities of dance.

Motivation: The poem is read several times by different people, or in some circumstances it could be accompanied on percussion instruments by the teacher (in which case she must know the poem by heart and have practised the accompaniment). More intensive stimulation may be achieved by this means, or the musical imagination of the children could be aroused.

Once the poem has become thoroughly familiar to the children, several questions and suggestions will arise:
— Why are the children dancing in this poem? — Why do they dance in one way and then quite differently? — What kind of music produces stiff movements? — What kind of instruments produce such music? — What do movements that are flicking, swooping, sweeping, trailing etc., look like? — When the rhythm changes, must the movement also change?

Experiment: The tasks arise out of the questions and inspiration of the children. They decide for themselves who wants to experiment first with the music or with the dance.
Examples for tasks:
a) What kind of movements will clearly describe the first part?

"Children start moving in stiff movements

*Poem by Alex M. from 'Miracles' Poems by children of the English-speaking world, collected by Richard Lewis, New York, 1966.

198

A flicking in time movement, arms reaching, feet snapping
Bodies stiff."

The children's movements are short, chopped, often asymmetrical, jerky, seldom simultaneous in two limbs, mostly staying on one spot, hard, cramped, practically without contact with other children.

b) What music will be suitable for these movements?

Since there are likely to be many different suggestions much discussion will follow. It is often the case that it is not only the sound of the instrument, but also the way it is played and the kind of rhythm that can produce the characteristic effect. Woodblock, side drum with snare, ratchet, cymbal — the sound of which is stopped abruptly, drums with a bright, hard sound — are all possible. The music can be improvised throughout; contrary to the usual situation irregular rest lengths, unexpected accents, monotony of dynamics are being sought after as mediums of expression. Any synchronisation between movement and music is therefore purposely avoided in order to emphasise the "stiffness".

c) "The rhythm changes. . ."

Not only the rhythm itself, but the character of the music and also the instruments should change. A rhythmic ostinato using several instruments could be built up here. About eight children play on various percussion instruments (e.g. bass drum, possibly congas, two tambours at different pitches, claves, finger cymbals or Indian bells, maracas, woodblock, bongos). The first child begins with an ostinato on the lowest pitched instrument, the next joins in, also with an ostinato, when he has listened carefully and thought about the best timing for his sounds. So one child after another joins in until they are all playing complementary ostinati and listening attentively to one another. Over this two children, or the teacher and one child, can improvise a dialogue. As a contrast to the first part a swinging three-four time is recommended.

d) "Sweeping, swooping, gliding
Relaxed.
Fingers trail through the air."

As the contact and relationship of the instrumentalists is aural, so the relationship of the dancers must be visual. The movement must strive to provide the strongest contrast to what has gone before, e.g.: swaying, gliding, with impulse, simultaneous, often symmetrical, the whole body dances, travelling in space and contact with a partner develops, one could possibly allow some form of grouping to arise at the end (i.e. one large circle or two rows opposite one another).

e) "the drum ceases and movement stops"

The accompaniment can get quieter and quieter, or the instruments stop one after the other in the reverse order to that of entry. The movement becomes accordingly smaller and quieter until it comes to an end.

Summary: The children can work in small groups with an exchange of roles in order to give every child the chance of both dancing and playing an instrument. The individual versions can be shown to the other children and a critical discussion will result. In certain circumstances it may be necessary to decide whether the dancers or the musicians should give the signal for the change. Ideally the change should arise spontaneously and naturally through adaptation to one another.

The object of working at this theme is to deepen the understanding of the reciprocal influence of music and dance, and to develop ability in creating contrasts in both dance and music.

Notating sounds and gestures

This theme concerns itself with the problem of free notation and the various interpretations of such signs. For centuries the notation of movement and dance forms was a great problem. The mutability of this art is dependent upon the fact that for a long time it was only performed, and seldom transmitted, and then only partially, in a fixed form. Today there are various systems of notation of which 'Labanotation' and 'Benesh Notation' are at least known and used internationally.

Our theme is not, however, concerned with the introduction of objective symbols of a notation system, but rather tries to show a subjective creation and interpretation of certain graphic symbols. It is concerned with the reciprocal influence of gesture, sound and graphic symbol.

Preparatory exercises: To make the reciprocal action clear, the starting point should be changed frequently. A movement can be expressed graphically or musically, a graphic symbol can stimulate an acoustic and kinetic presentation, or different sounds can act as the source for a graphic or dance interpretation.

After some experimenting, most classes discover an abundance of possibilities. Out of this raw material of ideas it is sensible to choose only a few, contrasted motifs and to practise and refine them both technically and creatively.

1) Introduction: With her hands (leading with the palms, the fingertips, the elbows or the heel of the hand) the teacher draws an unbroken line in space. She can produce a horizontal line by travelling, or a vertical or diagonal line by bending and stretching. How can this line be reproduced through a succession of notes or through a sound? With a long sustained note that rises and falls in pitch or intensity according to the shape of the movement; through a 'static' cluster of instrumental sounds, etc. Who can draw the line on the blackboard or on large (prepared) sheets of paper?

2) Action – Experiment: Who would like to discover a motif, either acoustic, graphic or in movement? The others try to translate the given motif into the other two media. The children can perhaps work in threes or in small groups and the roles of initiating and translating must be shared. It is important for the children to discover which ideas transpose well, and why.

3) Reflection – Choice: By comparing the different solutions it is soon dis-covered that the simplest and clearest ideas are the most suitable.

Some examples:

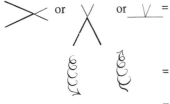 or = Touching oneself (hands, hand and foot etc.), a partner or the floor. The direction of the sign indicates the direction of the movement, the size gives the dynamic intensity.

= Spirals that show a rising or falling turning movement.

_ _ _ _ _ _ _ = Interrupted movement, the children decide on locomotion.

Instead of the examples given above each group of children should find their own symbols with stimulus and help from the teacher.

4) Creativity and working out: Work is continued in groups of three. The task is precisely defined:
a) Three motifs may be used and may be repeated in any order and as often as liked.
b) Each group should produce a graphic score that contains the arrangement of the graphic symbols used. It can be read from any side or in any direction if the authors wish.
c) The performers accompany themselves with appropriate sounds: Vocal – singing, humming, hissing, speaking with use of consonants and/or vowels; sound gestures, sounds made with the feet on the floor; instruments held in the hand while dancing, etc.

All other decisions are left to the performers.

Example for a solution:

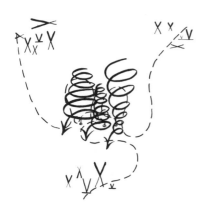

Phase 1:

Phase 1:
One child squats (sits, kneels) in each angle of a large triangle. One after another they start the touching motif, each one in a different way but all making a crescendo.
They accompany themselve with various explosive consonants (p,t,k,b,d,g), ending this move-ment motif with a strong accent.

201

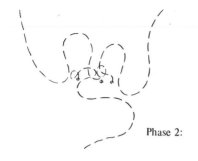

Phase 2:
Accelerando in various forms of locomotion (the gaps can become shorter and shorter but they should still be visible in a quick tempo) and at different levels to the centre of the space. Accompaniment with fricative consonants (sh, s, f, v, r, l). The gaps must also be acoustically clear.

Phase 2:

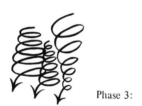

Phase 3:
When all three have arrived in the middle they start turning one after the other in quick succession in a spiral to the floor. Accompaniment through vocal glissandi on various vowels.

Phase 3:

5) Reflection – Summary – Critical appraisal – Further development: When the individual groups demonstrate their examples there should be a discussion about the inspiration and performance and perhaps about possible improvements. The suggestions of the other children as to how they would understand and interpret the individual graphic, acoustic and movement motifs show how many-sided are the creative possibilities of this theme.

Rhythmic rondo using instruments that are played while dancing

The tasks in this example stress three areas of activity: Playing instruments (percussion, recorders) while dancing;
The construction of a simple rhythmic canon;
The extension of this canon through improvised or prepared episodes into a rondo.
Several lessons will be needed to develop the theme fully.

Movement material: Step and close with change of direction, crossover step with turns, skipping, swinging walk in three-four time.

Instruments: Claves, tambours, finger cymbals, sleigh bells, recorders.

Development: If the children are playing instruments while dancing for the first time, or if it is a long time since they used them in this way, then the lesson will need to start with an opportunity to play with these instruments. Some of the

202

children may fetch the instruments that are lying ready; the others sit and watch. The children who are practising try out the best way of holding drums, claves, finger cymbals and sleigh bell anklets, if one wants to play them while dancing. They discover different ways of holding them and producing sounds. While doing this they can move on the spot or travel. They are free to choose how they move though they are advised in the beginning to limit themselves to some extent, e.g.

— The drum is alternately held high over the head (they then walk on tiptoe) or as low as possible (they remain standing).
— The sleigh bells, placed round the ankle, are best sounded through making many short, quick stamping steps.
— Finger cymbals are struck with a swinging arm movement.

The children who are watching may select the most interesting versions that should of course sound well too. After a while they change activities. All the children should be encouraged to try out different solutions.

Finally it is the turn of the recorder players. A limited range of notes is determined for them, for a first attempt a pentatonic scale is best. All those who are watching play a quiet ostinato (patschen and clapping) that sets the tempo. The players soon discover that while playing a recorder they cannot attempt any lively jumps. Quiet walking (possibly also swinging walk) is the most suitable.

After all these experiments the ways of holding* the individual instruments are once more discussed, explained and tried out. After a while they change activities.

The children now work at the rhythm of the canon:

To give the children an idea of tempo, phrasing and dynamics the teacher plays the whole sequence. The following suggestions may help with the teaching of this rhythm.

— Echo-play: The teacher first claps two bars at a time, the children taking up the echo immediately. Later they can manage four bars at a time.
— If they can use French time names, these can be included together with sound gestures to help memorise the sequence.
— The rhythm is written on the board, quietly read by the children and finally spoken or clapped.

After several repetitions, once the rhythm has been securely learnt, all tambours and claves are given out so that the canon can be practised. The drums start the rhythm notated above; the claves start it one bar later.

*See Appendix in *Elementaria* by Gunild Keetman, Schott, London, 1974.

203

Working out the movement form: The sequence of steps is practised without instruments. The children stand in one or more rows. The path for each child is a small square. Starting in the first bar with the left foot they take four steps forwards, the last (r) is a close; in the second bar (starting with the right) four steps to the right (using either step and close or cross-over step); in the third bar (starting with the right) four steps backwards, the last (l) is a close; in the fourth bar (starting left) four steps to the left (step and close or cross-over), the last (r) is a close with transfer of weight. (In the first and third bars the close is without transfer of weight, in the second and fourth bars with weight.)

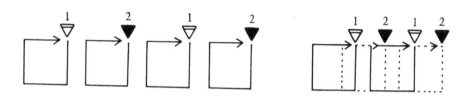

The distance from one child to another is at first so large that their paths do not cross. Later they are so close that their floor patterns in the canon do cross, on paper, though in performance the children do not meet, for the 'ones' are already moving sideways as the 'twos' start moving forwards. The performance in canon needs some practice. The steps should remain the same size in every direction.

In the second part a new motif is introduced: a turn is made (right shoulder leading backwards); each step takes one crotchet, with more skilled children a quaver. For beginners this is executed by a step and close on the whole foot, for the more skilled by cross-over steps (right on the whole foot, left on the ball of the foot). In the first bar turn to the right: in the second bar turn back to the front and stamp three times on the spot (r,l,r) — the drum can be held high for the four drum beats; in the third bar begin a turn to the left; in the fourth bar three stamps (l,r,l) to the two drum beats.

Grouping possibilities:
— One row stands diagonally across the room, either all facing the same way (a) or alternate children facing the front and back (b).
— Two rows facing one another (c).
(Drum and claves players alternate in each layout.)

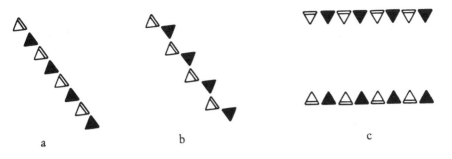

a   b   c

The canon can be worked at for its own sake or it can be used as the theme for a rondo.

Suggestions for working out rondo episodes:

B part: All players of the canon (with drums and claves) kneel on one knee and play a quiet ostinato on the claves and on the drums which they have laid down on the floor. Some recorder players form a chain and are led in and out of those playing the ostinato. The melody is already familiar having been prepared in the recorder lesson. e.g.

A melody can also be improvised by a child while the others play a melodic ostinato.

C part: Two or three children improvise with sleigh bells tied round their ankles. When using this instrument in this way the steps made must be very precise. Variety of sound can be achieved through steps on the ball of the foot or on the whole foot, through sliding steps and small jumps.

D part: A child with finger cymbals in his hands runs and turns in three-four time, accompanying himself with the cymbals. The movement path can be predetermined or it can be improvised by the child on the spur of the moment. If there are other cymbals at different pitches available, several children can take part in this episode.

The final form of our rondo consists of:
A Rhythmic canon with claves and drums
B Recorder improvisation in a chain
A Canon
C Improvisation with sleigh bell anklets

A Canon
D Improvisation with finger cymbals
A Canon

Simplification: With inexperienced children the canon rhythm can be executed in unison. Instead of a seven part rondo a three part form A-B-A or a five-part rondo can be given.

Dance song

This dance song from Carl Orff's 'Music for Children', Vol. 3 p.69 demonstrates a form very similar to a folk dance and one that a large group of children can learn in a short time.

Preparatory exercises: The children walk (run, skip) freely round the room; at a signal from one of them the others form a chain behind him.

Variation: The teacher, while providing a rhythmic instrumental accompaniment, calls out two or more children's names (according to the total number) and these children become the leaders of several chains.

The accompaniment is now played on a pair of bongos. When played on the higher pitched one a chain is formed (with or without holding hands), when on the lower one the chain is formed into a circle. When changing from circle to chain the circle is always broken on the very first note at a different place so that a different child leads the chain.

The children have formed more than one chain, each with about 6 – 10 children. The leader initiates a movement motif and the others imitate. After a while, or after a certain number of bars a different child leads. The improvisation is limited to step combinations made out of walking, running, bouncing, skipping, small steps, stamping steps with a downward emphasis or steps on the balls of the feet. Sound gestures can be added. The most important guideline in this exercise of invention is that the group must be able to take up the new motif immediately, i.e. it must be simple and clear.

Learning the song: If there is a music specialist the song and its accompaniment could perhaps be taught in the music lesson. If not then the song can perhaps be learnt as a unison song to a simpler form of accompaniment, and this could take place in the dance lesson.

Dance form:

A part – According to the number of children, several chains are formed, each with about eight children. They dance in various curves moving forwards. Their step pattern can be chosen from the more suitable examples invented in the preparatory exercises, perhaps a step, step, step, hop pattern as follows:

La la la la   la la la   la la   la la la   la la la la   la la la la   la la la la   la la
r,   l,   r,   r,   l, r,   l,   l,   etc.

At the end of the repeat of the first phrase each chain forms its own circle, facing centre. In the last bar, instead of the hop, land with both feet together.

B part – Continuous step and close to the right, in the seventh and eighth bars take three steps to turn to the right, the left foot closing to the right on the final beat.

La la   la la   la la la la   la la la   la la la la la la la la la la   la la la la   la la

These two parts can be repeated as often as is desirable. In the B part two chains (then more than two) form one circle until finally there is only one circle formed. After each B part different children lead the chains.

Variations: According to the skill and experience of the children the material can be varied, e.g.:

A part: Change of direction at the repeat so that the last child becomes the leader.

Different steps

B part: Cross over step, crossing alternately in front and behind, possibly with change of direction. At the repeat the cross-over steps could be bounced.

The camel and the monkey

A realisation in dance of one of Aesop's fables.

"In an assembly of animals the monkey stood up and danced. All eyes were turned to it and it was applauded with great acclaim. A camel, green with envy, wanted to receive the same applause. It got up on its hind legs and tried to dance also. But its movements were so grotesque that the animals became angry, turned on it and beat it and drove it away."

Motivation: In a preliminary talk with the children the behaviour of the animals, particularly of the monkey and the camel, is discussed. Why does the one dance and why the other? Do they have the same reasons for dancing? What is the reaction of the other animals?

It should be made clear to the children that fables are not just any old animal stories, but that they are a reflection of human behaviour and character transferred to animals. What could this story describe if it were about human beings? Have the children already experienced anything similar? How did they behave or how do they think one should behave? Some insight into the structure of social and psychological behaviour can be gained and experienced and transformed in play.

Questions of representation now arise. Which animals are present at this assembly, what do they look like and how do they move? (This theme could be prepared through a visit to a zoo so that the children can acquire enough material for observation.) How can one represent each individual animal so clearly that the other children know at once which one is meant?

Improvisation: Each child chooses the role of an animal, tries to find characteristic movements for that animal and makes suggestions for an appropriate musical accompaniment.

Once the introductory piece of music has been settled, and they have perhaps decided who is to represent the monkey and the camel by drawing lots, the story is run through several times in an improvisatory way. Every time notice is taken of suggestions, observations and criticism.

The teacher, and possibly two or three children who are musically inventive and fairly skilled, accompany on instruments. These are so organised that as many instruments as possible can be played by as few people as possible. The aim should be to provide very varied sound effects. Besides the usual percussion instruments use can be made of plucked string and wind instruments. Unconventional sources of sound and various pieces of apparatus can contribute to an unusual result. Different beaters and other auxiliary equipment must be prepared in advance.

Sequence of content: 1) A procession brings all the animals with their typical movements onto the stage, they collect and 2) the master of ceremonies greets them and shows them to their seats. The master of ceremonies could be a giraffe, an ostrich or some other such solemn animal. All greet one another and talk. 3) Suddenly the monkey gets up and starts dancing (music changes from the accompaniment motifs to a monkey dance). 4) The onlookers show great interest and applaud, taking the monkey to some place of honour. The more a fuss is made of the monkey, the more jealous and ambitious the camel becomes. 5) It tries to show itself off, prances awkwardly about, tries to jump and turn like the monkey, but its attempts at elegance fail utterly, all its movements are pitiful and grotesque. The assembly becomes restless, starts to make sounds of disapproval, becomes angry and 6) finally drives the camel away with scorn and derision.

After every run-through the interesting new ideas are retained and attention is given to the clarity of the miming. One has to exaggerate to make typical characteristics obvious to everyone.

e.g.   — The crocodile slides along forwards on its stomach, the two arms stretched forwards form its jaws and the spread fingers of both hands the dangerous teeth. Apart from individual lightening-quick reactions the movement is slow.

     — The kangaroo starting position is squatting. It moves forwards with big jumps. The typical holding position of the front legs must be taken into consideration.

     — The cock flaps excitedly and irregularly with its wings (arms), when crowing it throws its head back.

The children confirm that the better one knows animals and their movements the easier it is to represent them satisfactorily.

For a run-through within the framework of a lesson it is possible to work from improvisation to a loosely organised structure with many changes of role, with improvised music and an improvised text for the master of ceremonies. For a more detailed and carefully thought out performance some teamwork (dance and music teacher) and preparation is necessary.

Suggestion for an outline of scenes.

Scene   Music

1) Procession of the animals

The animals come from all sides, each moving in its characteristic way; they form a random group.

March, 4/4 time, over a rhythmic ostinato; all the instruments that represent the individual animals should be sparingly used.

2) Introduction – Master of Ceremonies

Each individual animal is proclaimed by the master of ceremonies: each one parades itself, bowing in all directions, and goes to its allotted place. Solos for the individual animals.

Repeated, short motif, e.g. various percussion instruments: timpani, cymbals. Recitative of the master of ceremonies. For each animal an appropriate instrument (or small group). Motifs must correspond to the movement in tempo, character, tone colour, rhythm and dynamics.

3) Monkey-dance

The monkey dances the 'well-known' monkey-dance, once round the spectators, then some special feat, another round, more new tricks etc.

A small rondo. "A" part, chromatic melody with accompaniment. "B" part accompanied by individual instruments with special sound effects (Swanee whistle). The A part remains the same length, the B part adjusts to inventiveness of monkey.

4) Applause

All applaud with beaks, front and hind legs, wings, tails, etc. All excitedly surround the monkey who proudly takes the seat of honour awarded him.

Only supported by sound gestures, possibly small percussion. Each time the monkey bows, suddenly very soft, then new crescendo.

5) Camel dance

Slow and intermittent in movement, interrupted through the camel's bows to all sides, and later through its own stumbling.

Music with many rests, shrill glissandi and short fragments of melody.

6) Expulsion

First watching, then head-shaking, anger and then expulsion. Small, cheeky animals most active, the clever old ones only shake their wise heads.

The most unusual sounds possible — rubbing taut balloons, shaking bunches of keys, whistling, Swanee whistle.

7) Epilogue

All the animals draw together into one group with morally disapproving raised forefinger. Exit to all sides.

Rhythmic speech chorus using a suitable proverb, e.g.: 'Be not envious of your neighbour's attainments'.

A small animal runs back and says:

'Everyone excels in something in which another fails.'

Glossary

Barred percussion instruments: Instruments with tuned wood or metal bars such as xylophones, glockenspiels and metallophones — sometimes called 'tuned percussion' or 'pitched percussion'.

Bouncing: This seems to be the nearest equivalent for one word to cover all the uses of the German word 'federn' in the context of movement. To understand its use here please turn to the detailed description on p. 82ff.

Change step: Unless clearly stated otherwise, in this book this term always refers to the rhythm quaver, quaver, crotchet — executed r, l, r, or l, r, l, according to context.

Child: Described throughout as "he" to distinguish him from the teacher who is more often a woman than a man in the case of the age range under consideration.

Crotchet: A quarter note (U.S.)

Dynamics: It is more usual to find this word in a purely musical context. For the special meaning intended here in relation to movement see p. 75.

Free leg: The one that does not bear weight but is passive.

Imaginative stimuli: Verbal suggestions of imaginary situations that may help to achieve the desired type of quality of movement.

Minim: A half-note (U.S.)

Nursery school: Here this term covers kindergarten, play group, pre-school, and represents the stage of organised play prior to recognised schooling.

Patschen: This term is used extensively in Orff-Schulwerk and is the German word for that sound gesture that is variously described as knee or thigh, slapping or patting. It denotes a flat-handed slap on the thigh near the knee. It requires a relaxed posture and can be executed when standing with feet slightly apart, or when sitting.

Primary school: The first stage of recognised schooling. In England this starts in the Infant or First school at five years, in most other countries at six years, and finishes in the Junior school at eleven years.

Quaver: An eighth note (U.S.)

Secondary school: This stage of schooling starts at eleven or twelve years and ceases when work or further education (college, university) begins.

Sound gestures: This term includes the sounds made by clapping, stamping, finger-snapping and patschen (q.v.).

Supporting leg: The leg that bears the weight of the body.

Teacher: Described throughout as "she" since more women than men teach children of the age range under consideration.

Working leg: Does not bear the weight of the body but performs an action.

Bibliography

Anatomy – Kinesiology
Duvall, Ellen Neal: *Kinesiology – the anatomy of motion*, Prentice Hall Inc.
Englewood, New York 1959
Todd, Mabel Elsworth: *The thinking body*, Dance Horizons, New York 1937

Choreography
Ellfeldt, Lois: *A primer for choreographers*, National Press Books, Alto Palo,
California 1962
Humphrey, Doris: *The art of making dances*, Holt, Rinehart & Winston,
New York 1960
Horst, Louis: *Modern Dance Forms*
– *Pre Classic Dance Forms*, Kamin Dance Publishers 1960
Russell, Caroll: Impulse Publications, San Francisco 1961
Turner, Margery: *New Dance*, University of Pittsburgh Press 1971

Dance and Art in general
Chujoy, Anatole and Manchester, P.W.: *The dance encyclopedia*, Simon &
Schuster, New York 1967
H'Doubler, Margaret: *Dance – a creative art experience*, University of Wisconsin
Press, Milwaukee 1968
Langer, Susanne: *Feeling and Form – a theory of art*, Routledge and Kegan
Paul, London 1967
Leeuw, Gerardus van der: *Sacred and profane beauty – the holy in art*, Abingdon
Press, New York 1963
Martin, John: *The modern dance*, Dance Horizons, New York 1965
Sheets, Maxine: *The phenomenology of dance*, University of Wisconsin Press,
Milwaukee 1966

Folk dance, country dance, play-party games, games
Botkin, B. A.: *Treasury of American Folklore*, New York Crown Publishers,
1954
Gomme, Alice B.: *The traditional games of England, Scotland, Ireland*, Dover,
New York 1964
Lawson, Joan: *European folk dances*
Newell, William W.: *Games and songs of American children*, Dover, New York
1963
Sharp, Cecil: *The country dance book*, vols 1 and 2, Novello, London, reprinted
1972
Wuytack, Jos and Aaron, Tossi: *Joy – play, sing, dance*, Leduc, Paris 1972

Historical Dance
Dolmetsch, Mabel: *Dances of England and France,* Routledge & Kegan Paul 1959
- *Dances of Spain and Italy,* Routledge & Kegan Paul 1954
Wood, Melusine: *Historical dances,* The Imperial Society of Teachers of Dancing. London 1956
- *More Historical dances,* The Imperial Society of Teachers of Dancing, London 1966

History of Dance
Haskell, Arnold L.: *The wonderful world of dance,* Doubleday & Co., Garden City, New York 1969
Reyna, Ferdinando: *A concise history of ballet,* Thames & Hudson, London 1964
Sachs, Curt: *World History of the Dance,* Bonanza, New York 1936
Sorell, Walter: *The dance through the ages,* Grasset & Dunlop, New York

Modern educational dance
Bruce, Violet: *Dance and dance drama in education,* Pergamon Press, London 1965
Bruce, Violet and Tooke, Joan: *Lord of the Dance – an approach to religious education,* Pergamon Press, London 1966
Caroll, Jean and Lofthouse, Peter: *Creative dance for boys,* Macdonald & Evans, London 1969
Doll, Edna and Nelson, Mary Jarman: *Rhythm today,* Silver Burdett Co., Morristown, New Jersey 1965
Eastman, Marcia: *Creative dance for children,* Mettler Studios, Tucson, Arizona 1954
Grey, Vera and Percival, Rachel: *Music, movement and mime for children,* Oxford University Press, London 1964
Jordan, Diana: *Childhood and Movement,* Blackwell, Oxford 1966
Laban, Rudolf v.: *The Mastery of Movement,* Macdonald & Evans, London 1960
Lockhart, Aileene: *Modern dance – building and teaching lessons,* Brown Company, Dubuque, Iowa 1957
Lofthouse, Peter: *Dance – activity in the primary school,* Heinemann educational books, London 1967
McKitterick, David: *Dance,* MacMillan, London 1972
Mettler, Barbara: *Basic Movement Exercise,* Mettler Studios, Tucson, Arizona 1972
- *Materials of Dance,* Mettler Studios, Tucson, Arizona 1960
Murray, Ruth Lovell: *Dance in Elementary Education,* Harper & Row, New York 1963
North, Marion: *A simple guide to movement teaching,* London 1964
- *Personality assessment through movement,* MacDonald & Evans, London 1963
Preston, Valerie: *A handbook of modern educational dance,* MacDonald & Evans, London 1963

Redfern, Betty: *Introducing Laban art of movement*, MacDonald & Evans, London 1955
Russell, Joan: *Creative dance in the primary school*, MacDonald & Evans, London 1965
— *Creative Dance in the secondary school*, MacDonald & Evans, London 1969
Movement, Dance and Drama — Report of the Conference of the University of Hull, 1970

Notation
Benesh, Rudolf: *Introduction to Benesh Notation*, Black, London 1955
Causley, Marguerite: *Introduction to Benesh Movement Notation*, Max Parrish, London 1967
Preston-Dunlop, Valerie: *An Introduction to Kinetography Laban*, Macdonald & Evans, London 1966
— *Readers in Kinetography Laban*, Macdonald & Evans 1966

Poetry
Baring-Gould, W. and C.: *The annotated Mother Goose*, Clarkson N. Potter, New York 1962
Fowke, Edith: *Sally go round the sun*, McClelland & Stewart, Toronto 1969
Leaf, Munro: *The story of Ferdinand*, Hamish Hamilton, London 1937
Lewis, Richard: *Miracles — Poems by children of the English-speaking world*, Simon & Schuster, New York 1966
— *Journeys — Prose by children of the English-speaking world*, Simon & Schuster, New York
Opie, Iona and Peter: *The lore and language of school children*, Oxford University Press, London 1959
— *The Oxford Nursery Rhyme Book*, Oxford University Press, London 1957
Withers, Carl: *A rocket in my pocket*, Holt, Rinehart & Winston, New York 1969
Woodland, E.J.M.: *Poems for Movement*, Evans Brothers Ltd., London 1966
Worstell, Emma: *Jump the rope jingles*, Macmillan, New York 1961